50

SIMPLE ⊞ WAYS ✂ TO MAKE LIFE SAFER FROM 🏠 CRIME

Susan Hull

POCKET BOOKS

New York   London   Toronto   Sydney   Tokyo   Singapore

The author has gathered the techniques and suggestions presented in this book from law enforcement agencies, security companies and other similar sources. Criminals, particularly violent criminals, are unpredictable and may not react as expected in given situations, and suggested preventive and responsive measures may not be effective in all circumstances. Care should therefore be taken when following the author's suggestions. The Publisher does not warrant or endorse the techniques and methods presented in this book. The Author and the Publisher assume no responsibility for any injury or damage to persons or property which is incurred as a consequence, directly or indirectly, of the use and application of any of the contents of this book.

An *Original* Publication of POCKET BOOKS

POCKET BOOKS, a division of Simon & Schuster Inc.
1230 Avenue of the Americas, New York, NY 10020

Copyright © 1996 by Susan Hull

ISBN: 0-671-52712-6

First Pocket Books printing October 1996

10 9 8 7 6 5 4 3 2 1

POCKET and colophon are registered trademarks of Simon & Schuster Inc.

Text design by Stanley S. Drate/Folio Graphics Co., Inc.

Printed in the U.S.A.

CONTENTS

GATHER YOUR FORCES
Tips for Anyone, Anytime, Anywhere

Contents

Contents

❖

TEACH YOUR CHILDREN WELL
Tips for Safer Kids

❖

Contents

◆

A FEW SIMPLE TOOLS
Tips for Protecting Property

◆

Contents

OUT AND ABOUT
Tips for Safer Comings and Goings

Contents

◆

OUR GREATEST FEARS
Tips to Consider
When All Else Fails

◆

◆

REAL COMMUNITY
Tips for Creating Permanent Solutions

◆

Contents

INTRODUCTION

◆

Crime—What Can *You* Do?

If, for very little money and almost no effort, you could dramatically reduce your spouse's (your employees', your friends', your own) chances of becoming a victim of crime, would you do it? Would you do the same for your kids? Sure you would. How about for your home, your car, your business?

Polls tell us that in the United States of the '90s, the number one concern of the average citizen is crime—protecting ourselves from an ever-increasing menace that seems to affect us all. With such polls in mind, some U.S. crime statistics become almost impossible to believe: In thirty percent of all burglaries committed, for example, the thief made his entry *through an unlocked door or window!* A crime is reported every seventeen seconds in this country, yet it's estimated that *only about half the crimes committed get reported at all!* We think that violence occurs at random, committed by the bad people we call criminals, but the truth is that the vast majority of violent crimes are committed by someone we know—*family and acquaintance assaults, rapes, and murders account for most of those crimes.*

In the course of researching the material for this book, I've come to believe—as do many experts—that your own intelligence and good sense are your greatest protection, and that action, in and of itself, makes you more powerful. That is what this book is about.

In spite of a lifestyle and habits I considered "safe" by any standard, I was the victim of three serious crimes during the last decade—a brutal assault, a hotel room "cat" burglary while I slept, and a relentless stalking for several years. One day in 1993 I realized that my fundamental reality now included a generalized fearfulness far greater than what should be any citizen's reasonable concerns about crime. In response, out of outrage and a refusal to accept fear as a fact of life, I resolved to change it, to discover what I could do—on my own—to "crime-proof" my life, including my family, my home, my travels, my belongings.

I sought the advice of experts of all kinds and found dozens of very simple things we can each do to help reduce our vulnerability to crime. I learned that many tips offered by law enforcement, security experts, self-defense experts, and others are not at all difficult to do and may not only help us *feel* safer, but truly *be* safer. And it's information that applies to everybody.

Most importantly, I found that DOING something was the key to changing the odds. Implementing what I learned has tempered my fear and replaced it with confidence. In every way, I am safer than I have ever been. This book is about empowerment *without* succumbing to paranoia or imprisoning yourself in fear.

Many ways to reduce our chances of being a crime victim are so obvious they seem almost silly—simple, commonsense measures. Others are less obvious, but many of the BEST ways to protect ourselves are easy, cost little or nothing, and can be done *right now* by any average person. In this book you'll find simple tips without the philosophy, the statistics, the debate, or explanation that fills most books on crime prevention, and without having to sift through hundreds of pages to answer the question "What can I do, right now, in *my own* life?"

Many excellent books are available that study crime and crime prevention in all of its aspects or cover a particular kind of crime at length. In this concise format I haven't tried to do either but rather to offer you ideas, based on solid information from experts, to get you started. For anyone with specific concerns or interests beyond the scope of this book, I encourage you to seek additional information and instruction.

There are no guarantees in life, and certainly no

guarantee that you will never become the victim of a crime, but the suggestions in this book will start you toward greater security, with concrete, how-to information that can help make your life—and the lives of people you love—safer.

My sincere thanks goes to the dozens of people who supported this project with resource materials, advice, or an inside view of problems faced by law enforcement and private citizens. I am grateful for friends and family who gave freely of encouraging words and intelligent comment. To Jane, my heartfelt thanks for your confidence.

Predictably, I encountered "the pronoun problem" in this book. There's no good way to solve it, so although not all criminals are men nor rape victims women, I used the male and female pronouns throughout to represent a majority of instances and broke rules of grammar occasionally by using "they" where a singular pronoun belongs.

This book is intended to be accessible to everyone, children included, and for that reason I've tried to avoid using language that is scary. One of the questions I hear frequently is, How can we teach good crime-resistance skills, especially to children, without imparting fear and distrust? There are no easy answers, but I believe that adults can have their most positive influence on children by having a matter-of-fact, pragmatic attitude themselves. Think of crime resistance as you do planning for fire or for earthquake or flood, and include it along with general emergency planning. Children will more than likely mirror your attitudes, so the place to begin is within.

You'll learn at least fifty ways to make life safer from crime by reading this book. Find those that apply to you, and DO them. The real secret to taking back our lives from crime is in the DOING.

GATHER
YOUR FORCES

❖

Tips for Anyone,
Anytime, Anywhere

TAKE CHARGE

Resolution is the first step

There is something mighty about intent—your own ability to decide how things will be. Much of the power you'll reclaim by doing these fifty simple things comes from your firm commitment to do something—no more excuses, no more waiting for somebody else to fix things, no more "tsk-tsk, isn't it awful?" You've

> AS YOUR FIRST, MOST POWERFUL ACT,
> DECIDE RIGHT HERE AND NOW THAT
> YOU WILL <u>DO</u> THE SIMPLE THINGS
> AVAILABLE TO YOU TO MAKE YOUR LIFE
> SAFER FROM CRIME.

already set things in motion by picking up this book. Now make up your mind—the most powerful crime-prevention weapon you will ever possess—that you will no longer accept fear and vulnerability as a fact of life.

SIMPLE THINGS TO DO:

• Work to build confidence in yourself and your family. Virtually all experts agree that your best defensive tool against ANY kind of crime is your own mind. Knowledge, awareness, and prudent good sense will make you safer. That's true for everybody, kids included.

• Know the facts. Most of us are HUNDREDS of times more likely to have something stolen than to become victims of violence. But of violent crimes, most are not the random acts of a stranger; the vast majority are committed by someone we know. Resolve to learn the realities of the problems you face and adjust your fears accordingly.

• Have a plan. Criminals have a plan, and they've thought about what they'll do. They count on victims to be unprepared. Eliminate their ability to surprise you by learning all you can now, before trouble happens.

• Remove opportunity. Most crimes are crimes of opportunity. Much of what you'll learn here is how to remove the opportunity that invites crime.

◇ **2** ◇

TAKE STOCK

Preventing crime is a family affair

Many Americans name crime as the greatest concern of their daily lives—a pretty sad state of affairs.

We know that knowledge is one of the keys to feeling and being safer—learning all we can learn about what's really happening and what we can do about it. We also know that conscious action gives us power—we are more in control of things when we are

---

> GATHER YOUR FAMILY TOGETHER FOR
> A DISCUSSION OF YOUR CONCERNS
> ABOUT CRIME, AND TOGETHER BEGIN
> TO UNDERSTAND WHERE AND HOW
> YOU NEED TO TAKE ACTION.

---

doing something than when we are passively waiting for something to happen.

The place to start is by examining our concerns and those of our family—what is really going on around us, what are the things we need to change, what we need to learn more about.

SIMPLE THINGS TO DO:

- Family in this case also means any group of people who share circumstances or a set of concerns—your coworkers, your roommates, your neighbors, the members of your walking group. Include the children.
- Make a long list of all the problems you can name. Remember: No fear is silly. Understand that part of the process is airing complaints and frustrations about crime in general, about the police, about feeling powerless. Be patient with one another.
- If you don't know much about a specific crime you fear—how big a problem drug activity in your neighborhood is, for example—find out. Crime prevention officers or community relations officers from your local police department will be happy to help inform you about the local situation and will have excellent information on what you can do. Only by knowing exactly what problems we face can we begin to change them.
- Brainstorm ideas about ways you can better protect yourselves and your property—many of the best ways are just plain common sense. Talk about any weaknesses in your physical surroundings or your habits that might make you vulnerable. You'll be surprised

at the list you'll come up with. The tips in this book and other crime-prevention resources may alert you to areas of vulnerability you hadn't thought about. It's the act of doing that begins the process of taking our lives back from crime. Start now.

• If you're concerned about frightening kids, then make the meeting about family safety, and include fire protection and other safety matters. Kids can and should share in responsibilities of keeping home, family, and friends safer. By keeping your own attitude sensible and matter-of-fact, you will teach your kids to be rational, not fearful, about matters of security.

SURVEY THE SCENE

A planned inventory for homes and businesses

Police and sheriff departments want you to be safe from crime. To help, they offer a number of public services. One of the best is available almost everywhere simply by asking—a straightforward but comprehensive survey, room by room, point by point, for spotting weaknesses in your crime-prevention habits.

> YOUR LOCAL LAW ENFORCEMENT
> AGENCY OFFERS CRIME-PREVENTION
> INFORMATION AND ASSISTANCE AT NO
> CHARGE. CALL THEM TODAY FOR A
> POLICE CRIME SURVEY.

SIMPLE THINGS TO DO:

• Call your local police or sheriff at the office number (never call 911 for non-emergency business) and either make an appointment for a visit from a public information officer or ask to receive a printed form for conducting a survey yourself.

• If your local department can send an officer to help with your survey, gather some kids to participate. Teaching responsible anticrime attitudes is an ongoing process, so don't miss an opportunity for kids— including teens—to have positive, instructional interaction with a real cop.

• Bonded locksmiths or hardware stores sometimes have surveys you can conduct to better crime-proof your home or business. Remember, though, that they've got products to sell, so make your own considered decisions on recommendations that cost money.

• Many TV and radio stations have jumped on the bandwagon, too. Call them to ask for any printed leaflets or tip sheets they offer to the public.

• Next, gather your group together and review the weaknesses you've discovered. See #2, Take Stock.

ASK McGRUFF

Action begins with information

If you know a kid, you probably know McGruff, the dedicated "Take a Bite Out of Crime" national spokesdog of the National Crime Prevention Campaign. He and his colleagues at the NCPC offer an astoundingly wide range of information on community

---

SIT DOWN TODAY AND WRITE THE
NATIONAL CRIME PREVENTION
COUNCIL. ASK FOR INFORMATION ON
WHAT MATERIALS AND RESOURCES
THEY HAVE AVAILABLE, AND MENTION
ANY SPECIAL AREAS OF CONCERN.
DO IT NOW.

---

crime and drug abuse prevention, training materials for policy makers, schools, and community groups, a mountain of educational materials, the most thorough directory of local crime prevention programs in the nation, and a comprehensive listing of at least 130 other organizations that can offer you further help.

This remarkable organization is the best single source of comprehensive support for Americans interested in crime prevention.

SIMPLE THINGS TO DO:

• Write the National Crime Prevention Council at 1700 K Street NW, Second Floor, Washington DC 20006-3817, or call 1-800-WE-PREVENT. Ask for their free catalog, which lists the numerous free and low-cost information booklets available. For a booklet in Spanish, call 1-800-727-UNETE.

• Have children write for a free comic book. It will start them thinking about important things kids can do. The address is McGruff, Chicago, IL 60601.

• When your packet arrives, follow up. Read everything. Discover what other individuals and communities have achieved in fighting crime. Share what you receive with friends and neighbors.

• Contact additional organizations and agencies whose addresses are listed—those whose specialty is in an area you're concerned about, or those nearby.

• If you're impressed by what NCPC is doing, send them a few dollars, fully tax-deductible. Even a small donation is a big help in the fight against crime.

• Remember that the more you learn, the safer you'll be. The process never stops.

CALL OPERATION ID

Sometimes it pays to advertise

An identifying mark placed prominently on your property makes the statement to a would-be thief that yours is a place where people are conscious of security. It can stop him in his tracks. It also makes it much harder to sell or pawn an item if it does get stolen.

In most communities, marking property is made eas-

TELL WOULD-BE BURGLARS THAT YOU
WON'T MAKE IT EASY FOR THEM. CALL
LOCAL POLICE TODAY AND GET
STARTED ON OPERATION
IDENTIFICATION.

---

ier by police departments and others who have marking tools to lend and thorough instructions to follow.

SIMPLE THINGS TO DO:

• Nearly all police and sheriffs' crime-prevention units sponsor an Operation Identification program and can give you solid instruction in how to better protect your property. They'll provide you with a kit or packet to use for marking and taking inventory of all the valuables in your home or business.

• Ask about marking equipment. In many communities, an electric engraving tool is available on loan at no charge from police or from the local library. Some police departments also have invisible ink markers for items that can't be engraved, such as furs, crystal, antiques, or art. A jeweler can mark jewelry for a small charge.

• If it's not available on loan, suggest that your block watch group, employer, or other group of concerned people buys an engraving tool to lend to its members. The tool is inexpensive and is available at hardware stores.

• Most police departments recommend using your driver's license number followed by your state's two-letter abbreviation as your identifying mark. If your state is one that uses social security numbers on driver's licenses, there is often a provision whereby you may request an alternative number. Do so; it is easy to get information on a person by using a social security number.

• Your mark should be placed prominently, where a

thief can see it or a pawn shop buyer will be alerted.

- Include items such as bicycles, tools, car stereos, etc., which normally aren't kept inside the house.
- Get the whole family involved. And while you're at it, get out the camera and photograph each item before you put it away, documenting serial numbers and other identifying information. Also photograph all four walls in each room and contents of garage, sheds, cupboards, and closets. Make notes as needed. Keep your documentation in a safety deposit box or other safe place outside your home. In case of loss of any kind, this will prove invaluable.
- If you're a senior citizen, call a local scout troop to help you and some of your friends. They'll jump at the chance.
- Advertise the fact that you've joined Operation Identification by using the stickers provided by police on windows and exterior doors.
- This is a good time to make sure your house number is clearly marked also, so you can be found quickly in any emergency.

MUM'S THE WORD

Sometimes it DOESN'T pay to advertise

You'll hear it said again and again: Most crimes are crimes of opportunity. Without thinking, it's easy to practically invite a criminal to come on in and help himself.

It's wise—and very easy—to drastically reduce the amount of information someone can use to commit a crime. It's mostly a matter of awareness.

KEEP PERSONAL INFORMATION

PERSONAL. LIMIT WHAT YOU SAY IN

PRINT, ON BELONGINGS, AND

IN CONVERSATION.

SIMPLE THINGS TO DO:

• Remove any identification on your key ring—your name, your address, your license plate number. If you lose your keys, you won't have the worry of leading a stranger straight to your door or your car.

• Carry your keys in a separate place from your wallet. Your address and the key to it are a risky combination.

• Use only a phone number, not an address, in a classified ad. And don't post an ad or announcement for your "big 50th anniversary party" or your "long-awaited cruise to the Bahamas." Houses that are open during celebrations or empty for vacations are easy targets.

• Be careful, too, of broadcasting information in a casual conversation with your supermarket checker or in the tavern where the team meets after the game. Anybody can listen in and use the information.

• When scheduling a repair or sales call, you don't have to explain why Tuesday isn't good, just that it isn't.

• After Christmas, a birthday party, or a delivery for your newly decorated bedroom, break down boxes or mailers and get rid of them. Boxes announce there's something new around.

• Women, seniors, singles: Use only your first initial and last name on your mailbox, in the phone book, or when you send for information, enter a contest, place an order. Old attitudes prevail, and criminals—not the most enlightened of thinkers—take notice of anything they interpret as vulnerability.

7

YOUR OPEN-DOOR POLICY

You decide who enters

It seems to be human nature to trust others, and most of the time people are as trustworthy as they appear. Still, we could pay a very high price for being wrong just one time, so it pays to establish good habits for determining how and when someone enters your home or business.

> MAINTAIN CONTROL OVER WHO
> ENTERS AND HOW. DEVELOP A SET OF
> RULES AND INSIST THAT EVERYONE
> PRACTICE THEM FAITHFULLY
> WHENEVER THERE'S A
> KNOCK AT THE DOOR.

SIMPLE THINGS TO DO:

• It needs to be said again and again—keep doors and windows locked.

• As you approach the door, yell "Honey, I've got it" or something similar, whether you're alone or not. You can use a similar ploy when you have a stranger in for a legitimate reason: "Just a minute while I lock the dog in the bedroom," "Will this be noisy? My mother is resting in the den," "I'll go get a check from my husband."

• Don't ignore a knock—it's like saying you're not home. Answer it verbally without opening the door. Open it only when you're certain of your visitor's identity. Listen to your instincts.

• Without opening the door, ask unsolicited salespeople to leave a business card in the mailbox. You can call them for an appointment if you're interested.

• Install a peephole and use it. They cost just a few dollars at a hardware store and take half an hour to install. Get one with a 190° viewing angle.

• Ask for a picture ID of service people, even if they have a scheduled appointment, and call the company to verify the name of the person they sent. Don't be embarrassed to do this—it protects them as well as you. Also, thoroughly check credentials of domestic workers, gardeners, and baby-sitters.

• Criminals sometimes impersonate police officers. It is prudent—and entirely acceptable to any real officer—to ask for photo ID and check badges carefully.

• Arrange to be on the phone with a friend when a

scheduled service person arrives. Your friend can hold while you give the worker instructions, then continue your conversation during the service call.

• Put away easily marketable items such as jewelry, cash, prescription drugs, documents, firearms, etc., before service or sales people, domestic workers, or baby-sitters arrive. Check valuables when they go. See #5, Call Operation ID.

• Do not allow baby-sitters to have guests at any time.

• Tell a neighbor when you know you'll have any outsider working in your home, whether you are there or not.

• Be careful of revealing information about your schedule or plans in casual conversation. It's easy to forget what "stranger" means as we get familiar with a worker or baby-sitter. See #17, Stranger Danger.

• Do not go outside with an "inspector" or sales-person unless you are certain of their identity.

• Check the credentials of contractors or anyone who is bringing a crew in to do work. Use companies whose employees are fidelity bonded. Do a thorough inventory when work is complete, and do maintenance checks on all phone lines, electric circuits, and security systems. It is very common for wires or components to be damaged in the course of work.

• If someone at your door appears to have an emergency, leave the door closed and make an emergency call for them. If they need immediate assistance such as in a medical emergency, call 911 to get help on the way, then call neighbors to assist you in rendering aid.

• Put a table or chest just inside the door you routinely enter, then use it to put bags, briefcase, or parcels down while you close and lock the door behind you immediately.

• Door chains are NOT safe. Get rid of yours altogether and get sturdy dead bolts. Any false sense of security will go with it. See #28, Dead Bolt Do's and Don'ts.

HOUND 'EM

The oldest anticrime device still works

Though no alarm or defense device is 100 percent fool-proof, one that police and criminals agree comes close is the faithful dog, or even a reasonable facsimile. Whether you own the real thing or an imposter, following a few rules will make it work for the best protection.

THE PRESENCE OF A DOG IS

COMMONLY NAMED BY CRIMINALS AS

THE ONE THING THAT WILL ALWAYS

DISSUADE THEM FROM COMMITTING

A CRIME.

SIMPLE THINGS TO DO:

• Criminals avoid dogs, even small dogs, and even the suggestion of a dog. Yard signs saying "Beware of Dog" may serve to dissuade many criminals.

• Home security stores or "spy shops" carry an alarm which, when triggered, barks like a dog. With some versions, increased noise or force by an intruder will trigger more vigorous barking.

• If you own the real thing, you already have an excellent crime deterrent. Don't make the mistake of believing your dog must be vicious or must be "trained" as a watchdog to do the job. On the contrary, the best defenders are also the best pets—a dog who is well treated and educated in the basic commands of sit, stay, come, heel, and down is a dog who will alarm and defend based on his devotion to you.

• Poorly educated dogs are unhappy dogs and can be dangerous. If you own a dog, train him. Also understand that dog training is in reality owner training—learning consistency and discipline in the way YOU behave with your dog.

• Understand your dog's behavior. At heart he is a pack animal, and your basic teaching does more than train him to come when called. He learns that you are the pack leader to whom he looks for cues that will shape his attitude and behavior for a lifetime. He will naturally sound the approach of a stranger to his pack, and he should NOT be discouraged for barking in alarm. Rather, praise him, and let him know to stop when you have gotten the message. Dogs who bark indiscriminately have simply not learned well. Call a dog behavior specialist for help with problems or to learn basic commands.

- The generic pronoun "him" is used here only for convenience. Both males and females make excellent alarm dogs.
- Some breeds are particularly suited as alarm dogs. Call the American Kennel Club or a dog behavior specialist for information and suggestions. If you are an average family or homeowner, do NOT get a trained security dog—they are an entirely different kind of animal to be used only in very specialized situations.

PHONE FACTS

Control your communications

Phones are such a large part of our lives that we may not think of them as having any role one way or another in our efforts to make ourselves safer from crime. The tips that follow, though, could make a very BIG safety difference for your family or at your workplace.

> YOUR TELEPHONE IS A MAJOR
> CONDUIT OF INFORMATION BETWEEN
> YOU AND OTHERS. FOLLOW SAFE
> RULES FOR PHONES AND ANSWERING
> MACHINES JUST AS YOU WOULD FOR
> FACE-TO-FACE ENCOUNTERS
> WITH STRANGERS.

SIMPLE THINGS TO DO:

• Most of us know to simply hang up if we receive an obscene call. Also hang up—and teach kids to hang up immediately—if a call is a prank, a threat, or any kind of harassment whatsoever, or if a caller does not identify himself as soon as asked. Some experts recommend keeping a police-type whistle near the phone and blasting harassing callers.

• If knowing who is on the line BEFORE you answer is important to you, ask your phone company about Caller ID. It requires the purchase of a small device to display a caller's number (about $30–$80), but may be worth it if you are concerned.

• Your answering machine can also be used to screen calls. Anybody who needs to get through will speak to it, and you may answer if you choose to.

• Your recording should simply ask for a message: "Thanks for calling. Leave a message after the tone." We're all so used to these machines that long messages are simply redundant and too often give away clues; callers know you "can't come to the phone right now," and they know it's no indicator of whether you're there or not. More on machine messages:

–Don't use your name, your number, your schedule—"here weekdays 9–5," "usually home evenings." Never say you're not home or "will return Tuesday."

–Don't say "I" if you live alone. It's better not to use a pronoun at all, but if you must, use "we."

–Like it or not, women are perceived by many

criminals as more vulnerable than men. Some single women ask a man to make their recording.

• In the phone book, list only your last name, first initial. There's no need to list your address either.

• Don't give out information to wrong-number callers—"No, you've reached the Smiths at 555–4321." All they need to know is that you're not the person they called. Take note of too many hangup or wrong-number calls and alert police if something seems amiss. Burglars "case" a location in many ways, including by phone, so don't say anything more than you have to if you don't know the identity of a caller.

• Post your list of emergency phone numbers— police, fire, neighbor or friend, work numbers, etc.— near every phone in your home or business. Also include your own address so it can readily be given to emergency personnel by anyone calling from that phone.

• Post your house number clearly. Police on emergency calls often have BIG problems finding homes. Avoid delays by mounting numbers large enough and in a location where they can be easily read from the street. A variety of number styles and sizes are available at any hardware store.

• Do not participate in phone surveys. Just don't— you are giving information away to a total stranger.

• Similarly, never make a purchase or otherwise agree to a phone offer if you are the RECEIVER of the call, no matter how nice the seller seems. If you really want what they're selling, get a number, hang up, and call them back several hours later to verify it's a business, but KNOW that this is not a foolproof check.

• Leave your phone in service during vacations. The small cost you might save by disconnecting is not worth tipping a burglar to your absence. Also see #26, Two Places at Once.

• Here's the one tip in this book that costs more than a few dollars: Cellular phones can be a real help in an emergency, particularly in your car, but also at home. Costs are coming down. Look into it.

◇ |10| ◇

THE CREDIT CRUNCH

How to be sure your credit stays yours

We've all heard about credit card theft—somebody gets your card, or even just the number, and charges thousands of dollars before you know what's going on. It's on the increase, and it seems the criminals who do

> COMMON SENSE IS YOUR BEST ALLY IN
> PREVENTING CREDIT CARD FRAUD,
> AUTOMATIC TELLER MACHINE THEFT,
> AND OTHER CRIMES RELATED TO
> CREDIT CARDS. DEVELOPING GOOD
> HABITS IS THE KEY.

it are getting more clever. There are a number of ways credit theft can happen, but most of the time, the losses from this kind of crime can be prevented with a little awareness.

SIMPLE THINGS TO DO:

- Obvious cautions:

–Check your statement carefully each month. It's amazing how many people simply write a check for the payment requested and never look at the list of charges. Report a missing card or odd charges on your bill to the issuing bank immediately.

–Don't write your PIN number on or near your card, and don't use your birthday or social security number as a PIN.

–Cut up expired cards into little bitty pieces.

–Keep a list of all your credit cards, bank account information, loan information, etc., in your safe deposit box.

- Less obvious, be sure the credit slip is completely filled out and totaled before you sign it, and check that the card returned to you is the same card you gave. Switches have happened.

- Use your card number for phone purchases only when you know the company well, and only if you have placed the call yourself—NEVER when you are the receiver of a call. See #9, Phone Facts.

- If asked to provide a credit card number as a guarantee when paying by check, refuse and ask to see a manager. This practice is illegal and should be reported to your credit card company (their 800 number is often printed right on the card).

• Carry only the card(s) you know you'll need. Keep the rest in a secure place.

• Request that your credit slip carbons be torn up before they're discarded, or ask for them and shred them yourself.

• Be aware when renewal cards are due so you can report any delay. A month or more in advance of a card's expiration date, call the company's 800 number to learn the date new cards will be mailed.

• Most credit card companies can code your account so that you do not receive convenience checks that can be used for cash; simply call and request it. If you do receive them, keep them secure or destroy them before throwing away as you would any other blank check.

• Lending credit cards is a practice you should think twice about, but if you let a family member use yours, collect all receipts for purchases when your card is returned, and call the 800 number in a day or two to verify recent charges to the account.

• Before you throw them away, tear up ALL offers for new credit cards you do not use. When an account is "preapproved," it often requires only a signature or phone call. A simple change of address could send a valid credit card in your name to ANYBODY.

• Automatic teller machines have become frequent sites for crime and require special attention:

   –Don't use one that's isolated or is partially hidden by shrubs or walls.

   –Keep on walking if you see someone hanging

around or if anything feels peculiar. Trust your instincts.

–Be aware of onlookers while punching in your numbers. Stand close to the keypad to block the view when punching in your account number.

–Take your receipts with you.

–Put away cash and card before you leave the window. Do it quickly; you can arrange things later. Note if anyone follows. ATM robbers have followed patrons and robbed them at their next stop.

◇ | 𝟭𝟭 | ◇

CON ARTISTRY

Stop fraud, scams, and swindles before they begin

Anybody can be the prey of a con artist, but most often this despicable thief preys on our elderly citizens, sometimes bilking them of an entire life's savings.

Police departments have issued warning after warning, but swindlers continue to find those who, worried about rising costs of basic necessities and concerned they may not have enough next month or next year, are especially vulnerable. All of us need to be aware, but

> YOU'VE WORKED HARD FOR WHAT YOU
> HAVE. PROTECT IT FROM SWINDLERS
> BY KNOWING HOW THEY OPERATE AND
> HOW TO SAY "NO."

if you are a senior, or know a senior, take time now to build protection BEFORE something happens.

SIMPLE THINGS TO DO:

• Have regular paychecks, social security checks, retirement payments, etc., deposited electronically to your bank account. You'll save yourself a trip to the bank, avoid exposure of any kind, and your checks will never wind up in the mailbox where they could be stolen.

• Pay for everything with a check or credit card—bills, groceries, purchases—and avoid carrying much cash. This is a pretty good money-management tip, too; you'll have a record of every penny spent.

• Know that con artists can be female as well as male. This is one crime where men do not vastly outnumber women.

• Make these rules inviolable:

–Never buy anything, sign up, or give out any information—not even your name—where you are the RECEIVER of the call. If you make it a rule, you will be certain never to be a victim of that particular swindle. Report any callers who will not freely provide you with information about their company. See additional tips on credit cards in #10, The Credit Crunch.

–ANY offers you are interested in—whether they come by mail, phone, or from your stockbroker—should be checked out. Any honest person will WANT you to be assured an offer is sound. Ask for literature, the company's history, written details of the offer. The Better Business Bureau or your state's attorney general's office can help. Never sign up without checking.

    —Never sign the same day. If you're told time is critical, don't do it, regardless of how convincing or how tempting it sounds. Remember the old saying? "If it sounds too good to be true, it probably is." It will be there later if it's legitimate.

• If you make a withdrawal from the bank for a significant amount, get a cashier's check or money order. Both are quite negotiable and much safer than cash.

• Be wary of street swindles. The schemes and the thieves themselves can seem very normal and very believable. Anyone who asks for money from you in a public situation should be reported.

• Don't be embarrassed if you fall victim to any of these schemes. Report it to police. Save any notes or paperwork. Alert local radio and TV stations so they can broadcast warnings to the community.

• Common schemes and swindles are numerous. Here are some to be aware of: work-at-home schemes requiring any investment from you, health or long-term insurance schemes, hearing aids or eyeglasses offers, remedies and cures for various ailments, claims against a debt you don't remember incurring, bargain prices on normally costly repairs or home improvements, any investment with a large expected return. Some may be legitimate, but you should check them out. Get more information from the police, the National Crime Prevention Council (see #4, Ask McGruff), or your Better Business Bureau.

TEACH YOUR CHILDREN WELL

❖

Tips for Safer Kids

MEMORY TRICKS

Kids' memories will serve them well

A part of every childhood are the wonderful word games played with parents from the very earliest years—nursery rhymes, the alphabet, and first numbers. Kids have an amazing capacity to learn by rote.

In addition to songs and games, children can remember a great deal of important information that could

> INSIST THAT CHILDREN OF EVERY AGE
> COMMIT BASIC INFORMATION TO
> MEMORY, BEGINNING WHEN VERY
> YOUNG. CONSIDER IT AS BASIC
> AS THEIR ABCs.

literally save their lives. Stress the importance of knowing certain things "by heart."

SIMPLE THINGS TO DO:

• Drill kids on the essentials until they know them. It's not hard to make a game of it. Beginning with simple name, address, and phone for preschoolers, you can increase the information they memorize as they get older.

• Here's what they should know by school age:
  –their full name and parents' full names
  –their full address, including city, state, and zip code
  –their home phone, including area code
  –the phone number of a trusted nearby neighbor
  –how to contact grandparents or a family friend
  –parents' work phones
  –how to use both dial and push-button phones
  –how to operate all locks, doors, and windows at home

• All children, regardless of age, should know how to dial 911 and speak understandably to the dispatcher. You can role-play this by thinking of situations, then using your phone with the receiver button taped down. (Make it very clear that this is never to be made into a game.) Practice as a family, even when kids are older.

• Be sure they know they can dial 911 from a public phone without a coin.

• Teach them what an emergency is, and when and to whom to tell the information they've memorized.

All children can learn to identify a police officer, a firefighter, etc. And teach them NEVER to give the information to anyone they can't identify. See #17, Stranger Danger.

- Practice. As every parent knows, kids forget.

IT'S A BIG WORLD

And you can't always be beside them

As parents, we have the enormous challenge of teaching our children where the balance lies between their natural openness and trust and a healthy dose of caution. It's not easy. And hardest of all, perhaps, is to

> JUST AS IS TRUE FOR ADULTS, MUCH ABOUT SAFETY IS IN KIDS' ABILITY TO USE THEIR OWN MINDS. TEACH THEM TO THINK SENSIBLY. LISTEN TO WHAT THEY TELL YOU. INSIST ON CERTAIN RULES.

teach them how to handle potential trouble when you're not there with them—at school, walking or pedaling to activities or friends' homes, all those times they're on their own.

SIMPLE THINGS TO DO:

• Teach these important lessons:

–Walk confidently and stay alert to what's happening around them. Most of the tips in this book apply to kids as well as adults. See #38, Walking Tall.

–Stick with friends. There's safety in numbers.

–NEVER get in a car with anyone they don't know. Never hitchhike, and for older kids, never pick up anyone.

–NEVER go in a public restroom alone.

–How to identify "friend" and "stranger." See #17, Stranger Danger.

–How to use a public or private telephone for emergencies, and how to remain calm. See #12, Memory Tricks.

• Let them know every day that they are important, useful, and competent. Give them a sense of belonging.

• At home, settle arguments with words, not with fists. Show kids by your example that letting an insult or rudeness go unchallenged is no big deal. Common courtesy is excellent crime-prevention strategy.

• Make your kids' friends welcome, and get to know them and their families. Make it known that yours is a home where kids can come for help. Write the National Crime Prevention Council for information on how to start a Safehome network in your area. See #4, Ask McGruff.

• Teens are the most frequent victims of crime and are at special risk. Keep them busy. Fill their extra time with positive activity by giving them specific responsibilities in your crime-prevention efforts. Channel their talent, spirit, and enormous positive energy in your community. Organize them to volunteer at school and around the neighborhood. See the last section in this book, Real Community, for ideas.

• Talk about drugs, openly and in detail—this is no subject to avoid. Get the facts—from schools, from police, from drug counseling centers. Agree in advance to stay relaxed and not lose your cool. Parents, make a point of listening at least fifty percent of the time; nothing turns a kid off faster than a lecture or accusations. Kids, tell your parents about feelings and experiences, and consider that your folks just might know what they're talking about. If you've got family communication problems, get help NOW. It's too important to ignore.

• Kids, keep your valuables in lockers, and don't share combinations. Lock bikes, and pressure schools to provide secure bike racks in open areas. Ask a parent to etch bikes with a mark of identification. Stay away from trouble spots—you know where they are. And think about the advisability of wearing expensive athletic gear. Fancy shoes and jackets have cost lives. Is looking cool worth that kind of risk?

◇ 14 ◇

HOME ALONE

A time to know the rules and follow them

Every parent would prefer to have responsible adult supervision for their children at all times, but the fact for many families is that the best child care is simply not logistically or financially available. Millions of "latchkey" kids attest to the reality, as well as toddlers being cared for by older siblings, and baby-sitters barely old enough not to need care themselves.

YOUR "HOME ALONE" KIDS WILL BE
SAFER BY HAVING A SET OF FIRM
RULES AND PRACTICING THEM
FAITHFULLY. INSIST ON IT.

SIMPLE THINGS TO DO:

• Agree upon a check-in procedure when kids arrive home to an empty house. They can call you at work or check with a neighbor who works at home.

• Kids should know how to work every door and window lock in the house and should check them regularly. This is a good chore for kids to do on a daily basis, and it develops the habit.

• Post all emergency phone numbers—police, fire, poison control, your work, a relative, a neighbor, plus your own address—near every phone in your house, and be sure relatives and neighbors have current information on how to reach you.

• Medical personnel are allowed to take only basic measures to keep a child alive without specific parental permission to render treatment. Anyone you designate to take over in an emergency—a relative, friend, or neighbor—should have a basic authorization from you granting permission for your child's care. Ask your attorney about wording. A typical one says, ''This is my authorization for Jane Smith to secure any urgent medical care for my children, James and Sharon Johnson, in my absence. (Signed) _____.'' If your child has a medical condition or takes medication, include that information.

• Basic home-alone rules should include:

  –No unauthorized guests. This goes for baby-sitters, too.

  –Doors and windows locked at all times.

  –Never open a door to someone they don't know and never say they are alone. Do not ignore a knock, either. Rather, say through the closed door, "My mom's resting," and call a neighbor who can look to see that the visitor leaves.

–Never tell a telephone caller they're alone. Even better, let an answering machine screen calls, or devise a signal (one ring, hang up, call back, for example), which they must hear to answer at all.

–Never enter the home if a door or window is ajar or broken. Go straight to a neighbor and call the police.

• Baby-sitters should know whom to call with urgent concerns—not just a true emergency—if you are unavailable, and they should follow the same "home alone" rules the kids do.

◇|15|◇

WAY TO GO

Take a family safety outing

We adults rarely venture farther on foot than the garden hose stretches, while kids walk the neighborhood every day, familiar with every hiding place, shortcut, and friendly dog.

We all tell our children to run from a threatening situation, but we rarely think to tell them where they can run TO. Taking the time to get to know your neigh-

> HAVING KNOWN AND PRACTICED
> ROUTES TO SAFE PLACES CAN GIVE
> YOUR KIDS THE CRITICAL EDGE THEY
> NEED TO ESCAPE FROM TROUBLE.

borhood from a kid's perspective can make an enormous difference in your children's safety.

SIMPLE THINGS TO DO:

• Walk kids' usual routes with them—to school, to the park, to friends' homes. Use your adult knowledge to note any trouble spots in the environments they pass through daily.

• Ask kids to stick to the same routes every day to school or their regular activities. Even though you should insist they don't use them, learn where the shortcuts are—kids ALWAYS know them, but adults rarely do.

• Know your kids' schedules and how long each trip takes, and act immediately to locate them if they are even a few minutes late. Make it clear to school and activity leaders that you want to be called immediately if your kids don't arrive. Time is everything when a child is in trouble. Kids may be embarrassed at your fast action, but they'll learn to call you if they're delayed, and they'll get the message you care.

• Walk, don't drive, to some of the businesses you frequent, particularly where you've gotten to know an owner or clerk, and make sure your kids know them, too. Learn the route together, on foot, to the police station nearest you, fire stations, 24-hour markets, anywhere there are people at all hours.

• Start a Safehouse program in your neighborhood. See #4, Ask McGruff.

• Finally, as a family, make a simple map of the

neighborhood, with routes marked clearly. Then begin taking walks as a regular family event, using the various routes to safety from time to time. You'll all have fun, and if anyone ever has to run for it, they'll find help quickly and automatically.

YOU SCREAM AND I SCREAM

Practice makes protection

As long as you've got the family together, now's a good time to practice this tried-and-true self-defense tool. For reasons that perhaps only psychologists un-

ONE OF THE BEST ALARMS—AND
OFTEN A GOOD DETERRENT TO A
PERSON WHO'S UP TO NO GOOD—IS
YOUR OWN VOICE, TRAINED AND
PRACTICED TO SCREAM. MAKE SURE
EVERY MEMBER OF YOUR FAMILY
KNOWS HOW, CHILDREN AND
ADULTS ALIKE.

derstand, many adults have trouble screaming—that high-pitched, ear-piercing scream we could all do as children but somehow forgot. Kids are perfect teachers of this valuable skill.

For most of us, it's just a matter of practice. While your mind is on crime prevention, take the time to learn or relearn how to let go a scream that can be heard a mile away.

SIMPLE THINGS TO DO:

• Somebody in your family or group can give a bloodcurdling demonstration. From there, it's mostly the willingness to try and keep on trying. You'll get it by imitating a screamer you know.

• Kids are great screamers, and they'll enjoy teaching you. Though your practice sessions may provoke some laughs, be sure children know the seriousness of your purpose, and caution them about screaming when there is no problem—remember the Little Boy Who Cried Wolf?

• While most kids are able to scream, some have been scolded for making noise of almost any kind. These kids need not only to learn and practice screaming but to be reassured that it is okay to scream if they are scared.

• Practice screaming words, not just noise. "AAAAA!" will get attention, but people hearing a scream may freeze in place if alarmed. Also scream "Stop! Let go! I don't know this man!" or "Call the police!" See #42, If the Worst Happens.

• Remember to warn any unsuspecting neighbors

about your practice plans, or go somewhere you won't be heard. A scream of the sort you're going to learn says "emergency" to anybody's ear, so take care not to alarm anyone unnecessarily.

• Keep in practice. Screaming is an important tool that one day could save you or your children from harm.

❖ 17 ❖

STRANGER DANGER

Friend or foe can look the same

It's as basic as a rule gets. Every parent in America has taught children not to speak to strangers, and most parents are pretty confident their children won't.

When it's put to the test, though, in city after city, state after state, we're finding that kids DO talk to strangers because they DON'T know what a stranger is. Kids think of a stranger as an ugly person, a creepy

---

CHILD MOLESTERS, KIDNAPPERS, AND

OTHERS WHO PREY ON CHILDREN

LOOK LIKE ANY AVERAGE PERSON. A

STRANGER IS ANYBODY—ANYBODY—

YOU DON'T KNOW WELL.

---

person, maybe a dirty person or frightening person. The truth is that most of the creeps who prey on children don't look strange, and our kids don't see them as "strangers."

Nothing could be more dangerous.

SIMPLE THINGS TO DO:

• Practice with your children identifying people they know and don't know. Help them to use "don't know well" instead of "strange" as their standard. Use pictures of a variety of people—you can make it a game while developing it as a habit. Use real events as discussion points—if you're asked for directions by someone, or if someone in the grocery line behind you says something nice to your kids, talk about it together afterward. Do we know that person well? What would you do if that nice lady asked for help? If she said "Your mom sent me"? If Johnny's brother's friend wanted you to go for a ride?

• Lures work on children. Common ones include asking kids for help (for directions, to find a lost puppy), telling them there's an emergency (their house is on fire, their mom has been taken to the hospital), hiring them to do errands, then having them come to a house or car to get paid. Drill your children over and over again on common lures, just as they do their arithmetic or alphabet drills.

• Write Child Lures, 2119 Shelburne Road, Shelburne, VT 05482, for information. Child Lures has compiled an inexpensive twenty-page family guide, endorsed by the American Academy of Pediatrics, which describes common lures used by child molesters and abductors and offers prevention strategies for each.

• Practice screaming and hollering "NO!" and make sure kids know it's okay to fight and kick if grabbed. See #16, You Scream and I Scream.

• It's critical that kids learn to rely on their own instincts. See #18, Belly Buttons. Make it clear that they must tell you if they have any encounter with someone they don't know or if they feel "funny" about someone.

• Also contact the National Center for Missing and Exploited Children, 2101 Wilson Blvd., Suite 550, Arlington, VA 22201, for valuable information and materials on a variety of issues involving children.

BELLY BUTTONS

Teach kids to trust what they know

There's one alarm that seldom fails us, but that we often fail to acknowledge. All of us, adults and children alike, have a powerful "gut instinct" we can rely on to tell us when something's wrong. Learning how is not just a good idea for kids, it's a good idea for everybody. In fact, it's essential.

> DETERMINING WHO AND WHAT IS
> "WRONG" IS NOT STRICTLY AN
> INTELLECTUAL PROCESS. HELP KIDS
> LEARN TO IDENTIFY THEIR BODILY
> RESPONSES—AND TO ACT ON THEM.

SIMPLE THINGS TO DO:

• Teach children to recognize the feelings that are their clues to what's okay and what's not. A funny feeling in their tummies can be an alarm they should trust and obey.

• Practice identifying these responses by asking kids what did they "feel" about a person they just met. Encourage them to describe their actual physical reactions—"warm inside" rather than simply "good," "skin crawly" rather than "bad." Have them point to the part of themselves that has the feeling.

• Be careful about brushing kids' feelings aside. An attitude that says, "You don't really hate Uncle Bob!" may deny a child his or her own valuable perception and may cloud your ability to see something important.

• Help kids define their own personal body space. Even very young children can understand "close enough to touch" and "close enough to talk to but not to touch." Teach them to retreat to maintain a safe distance if someone approaches their personal space without permission and role-play this for practice.

• Teach kids about good touching and bad touching, in terms of (1) acceptable areas of the body, (2) roughness, and (3) their own feelings about whether it's okay.

• Instruct children of all ages that there are no secrets from Mom or Dad. Don't ever ask them to keep a secret. Rather, call a hidden birthday present or a special announcement a SURPRISE. The word "secret" should be a trigger to tell Mom or Dad immediately.

• Talk to your kids about sex, starting early. There

is a sex "education" network on the street that you know nothing about, and your kids will be exposed to it no matter what you do, say, or think. Please don't send them out in ignorance to deal with this alone.

• Older kids need to watch their "belly buttons," too. Tell your girls it's all right to say no, to make a scene, to leave or call home for a ride at ANY time it no longer feels okay—even if things started out feeling fine. Tell boys the ONLY time it's all right to keep going is when they've heard a definite, verbal "yes." See #45, It's Not About Sex.

• Adults, you may have lost touch with your own belly buttons. Work on it. Developing a strong sense of what you feel and what your instincts tell you develops the most sensitive alarm anyone, young or old, can have for self-protection.

GOLDEN RULES FOR KIDS

Today's kids have more to learn

A few fundamentals will enormously increase kids' ability to deal with strange or scary situations. Special attention is paid in this book to specific circumstances, but some golden rules bear repeating again and again.

> A CHILD WHO IS CONFIDENT AND HAS
> PRACTICED RESPONSES TO
> EMERGENCIES IS A SAFER CHILD.
> CERTAIN RULES MUST BE FAMILIAR
> AND ABSOLUTE.

SIMPLE THINGS FOR KIDS TO DO:

• Memorize key information. See #12, Memory Tricks.

• On the PHONE, never say that you're alone, never give your name, address, or any other information. NEVER open a door to someone you don't know.

• NEVER follow along with a person you don't know, even if you are called by name, even if they say your parent sent them, even if they seem to need help.

• NEVER get into a car with a person you don't know very, very well and trust completely.

• NEVER go into a public bathroom alone.

• TRUST your feelings. See #18, Belly Buttons.

• You can say NO, even to someone you know. You can run away, you can scream, and you can fight if something bad happens.

• Settle arguments with WORDS, not fists, and avoid forming an audience when others argue. Groups and arguing don't mix.

• TELL AN ADULT you trust about anything peculiar that happens, anything wrong you hear about, anything odd you feel, any "secret" you're asked to keep. Trust that funny feeling in your stomach that tells you what "wrong" is.

• Stay in GROUPS. There's safety in numbers.

• KEEP TRACK of family members. Know one another's plans, schedules, whereabouts—even brothers and sisters.

• REHEARSE with your family and your friends what you will do in various kinds of emergencies.

GOLDEN RULES FOR PARENTS

Some tips to help you sleep more soundly

The old scout motto "Be prepared" is never more important than where you kids' safety is concerned. This is one area where an ounce of prevention can save a lifetime of heartache.

> YOU ARE THE SAFETY FOUNDATION
> YOUR KIDS STAND ON. TAKE THAT ROLE
> SERIOUSLY BY PROVIDING THEM WITH
> EVERY TOOL AVAILABLE. REINFORCE IT
> WITH YOUR ATTITUDE, TIME,
> AND ATTENTION.

Being involved in your kids' lives—even if they sometimes protest—gives them a solid base where they can feel sure and safe in their own lives and in your protection.

SIMPLE THINGS TO DO:

• Listen, listen, listen to what your kids tell you, and show them by your behavior that their thoughts and their concerns are safe with you.

• Make sure your kids know how to reach you wherever you are, and arrange for a trusted friend who will always be there for them as backup in case you are unavailable.

• Keep current pictures of your kids—how they look now—and update them regularly. Some police departments can provide you with a free Child Identification Kit.

• Know where your kids are at all times, regardless of their ages. Know the routes they take to school and to events. Know their friends and friends' families. Know the make and license numbers of friends' cars. Know when to expect your kids, and do not delay in calling police if something seems wrong and you cannot locate them.

• Don't mark a child's name prominently on backpacks, jackets, lunchboxes, etc. Names can be read from a distance and used by the wrong person.

• Speak well of police and encourage kids to get to know local officers.

• Set an example by refusing to buy stolen goods or

to use drugs, by reporting crime, testifying if needed, and acting in support of crime victims.

• Use courtesy always, and teach kids that manners are not only pleasant but can deflect conflict. Let insults roll off your back and kids will, too.

• Make it known that your home is a reliable, safe place for kids who are scared or need help. All kids need to know they have somewhere to turn for help no matter what. Form a Safehome network. See #4, Ask McGruff.

• Tell your kids again and again that if they are ever lost, you will find them, no matter what you have to do, how much it costs, or how long it takes. You will come.

A FEW
SIMPLE TOOLS

Tips for Protecting
Property

LIGHT FANTASTIC

Ways to brighten a criminal's day

Light is a criminal's worst enemy. The more there is, the more they hate it, and the less they'll want to stick around.

You can put an enormous dent in their plan and at the same time make your home or business more attractive, more valuable, and friendlier.

> BY ITS VERY NATURE, CRIME THRIVES
> IN DARKNESS AND ENCLOSURE,
> WHERE CRIMINALS CAN GO ABOUT
> THEIR BUSINESS UNDETECTED. MAKE
> YOUR ENVIRONMENT AS LIGHT AND
> OPEN AS POSSIBLE.

SIMPLE THINGS TO DO:

• Install bright lights around your entire home or business (a nighttime inspection will tell you where more light is needed). The new motion detector light fixtures are truly amazing. These fixtures are available for as little as $10, hold two adjustable floods to cover an enormous area, and light up automatically whenever someone comes within a distance YOU select. If you already have a fixture in place, you can buy just the motion detector.

• Increase wattage where fixtures already exist, and point flood-type fixtures to shine light in the most efficient direction. Some bulb types offer a range of choices to spotlight or broadly flood an area, so read package labels.

• Also inexpensive and easy-to-install are landscape lighting sets, which can fill in shadowy areas around bushes. Post-type fixtures push into the ground, connected by wire which is buried in a shallow trough.

• At night leave a light on inside the garage and in the house. From the outside, a light can say someone inside is awake and alert.

• When you buy an electric garage door opener, get one with a light that automatically comes on for ten minutes when the door is activated.

• Don't forget to light gates and walkways, hallways, stairways, laundry areas, and mailboxes in apartment buildings. If you're renting, pressure landlords to make these improvements—it's in their best interests, too.

♦ 22 ♦

WIDE-OPEN SPACES

Not just for homes on the range

For the same reasons they hate light, criminals don't like to operate where they can be observed by passing cars, pedestrians, or neighbors. Think about it—if you were going to do something illegal, wouldn't you look for a quiet, dark, private place to do it?

HIDING PLACES MAKE A YARD OR
BUILDING VERY ATTRACTIVE TO
CRIMINALS. BY REMOVING THEIR
ABILITY TO HIDE, YOU MAKE AN AREA
MUCH LESS APPEALING TO ANYONE
WITH BAD INTENTIONS.

Police know that the more light and visibility in an area, the less likely that area will be the target of crime. And some of the best ways to increase the visibility around your home or business require only a little labor and don't cost a cent.

SIMPLE THINGS TO DO:

• Get a friend or the kids to help you by trying to hide while you watch from the street and from a building's windows. You'll quickly spot problem areas.

• Trim back foliage and trees well away from windows, doors, or recessed areas. Trim bushes to two feet in height. You can still have bushy shrubs, but they won't effectively hide anybody. Cut tree limbs that allow access to windows or roof.

• Remove fences or barriers around trash cans, Dumpsters, or storage areas so view is unobstructed. Erect barriers to foot traffic passageways that provide escape.

• While you're outside, install a mailbox large enough to hold ALL your mail and newspapers, etc. A mail slot is even better. Get rid of that sign with the family name on it; some burglars like to call ahead to make sure you're gone. And make sure your house number is clearly visible from the middle of the street.

• See-through fences may sacrifice privacy but make a yard far less inviting to thieves. If you live in a high-crime area, consider it when it's time for a new fence.

• Visibility is especially important within three blocks or so of a major street, where burglars can quickly disappear in a crowd. A higher percentage of some kinds of crime happens near busy escape routes.

• Insist on regular maintenance of building and exterior and grounds if you're renting. Well-cared-for neighborhoods have less crime.

NUISANCE NOISE

Simple warnings you can rig yourself

One of the advantages a criminal has in many situations is the element of surprise—he knows what's coming, but you don't.

Hearing someone's approach can allow you to check

> NOISE IS ONE OF CRIME'S GREATEST
> ENEMIES AND CAN SEND TROUBLE
> RUNNING IN ANOTHER DIRECTION.
> THE MORE NOISE AN APPROACHING
> PERSON MAKES, THE MORE PREPARED
> YOU ARE.

if it's friend or foe, pick up the phone, take whatever action YOU decide. An unexpected noise can also startle an intruder enough to convince him yours is not the home or business he wants to enter.

Create an advantage for yourself and have some fun in the process. Kids love these tips. Get them involved.

SIMPLE THINGS TO DO:

• Hang small bells on inside gate handles, door-knobs, sliding windows, etc.—all entrance points where something must move. One- or two-inch brass bells like those you can buy during the holidays or year-round at craft stores work well and look decorative suspended from inexpensive brass chain. For outside bells, be sure they won't rust.

• No one can walk on gravel without making noise. Consider gravel walkways, entranceways, flowerbeds, etc. Some of the ground rock available from garden centers is colorful and decorative.

• Metal trash cans make more noise than plastic. Chain makes more noise than rope. You get the picture. When making any home improvement, think noise.

• Walk all around your home, apartment building, or business, down walkways, through gates, etc., to discover other places where noise could be used as a simple alert, then use your ingenuity to add bells, chains, anything that makes a sound.

FABULOUS FAKES

If he reads it, it must be true

There's much controversy about electronic security systems these days. The companies that sell them insist they reduce break-ins dramatically, and one study concludes you're three times less likely to be robbed with a system as without. At the same time, some police departments have had so many false alarms that they've stopped taking alarm calls seriously. And ex-

---

> HOW DOES A THIEF KNOW A HOME
> HAS ELECTRONIC SECURITY? HE SEES
> THE DECALS ON THE DOOR, THE SIGN
> IN THE YARD, THE WIRES ON THE
> WINDOW GLASS.

---

posés reveal that some of the time, at least, the security company's central system, which monitors the alarm and relays a call to local police, may be shockingly inefficient.

Still, if we could afford one, most of us would rather have a system than not, controversy notwithstanding. Experts agree that if a criminal has a choice, he will avoid a house he knows is equipped with electronic security alarms.

SIMPLE THINGS TO DO:

• Get a system if you can. Ask around. They may be more affordable than you thought. Your local police crime prevention unit may have valuable information on the types of systems available. If you choose to install a monitoring-type service, be sure the system will alert the monitoring company if your phone line is cut. Also, do not be misled by sales pitches that claim monitoring increases the chances of finding the burglar—it does not. The only function of a monitoring service is to notify police that your alarm is triggered. It is only as good as the speed and reliability with which it does that one thing and the speed at which police respond. Check into both.

• At the very least, buy the decals and yard signs from one of the independent surveillance stores or "spy shops" that have sprung up in major cities. Often you'll find an assortment, even fake cameras, sensors, etc.

• From a hardware or home improvement store, buy the tape security companies use for wiring windows—a thin copper wire on a narrow, clear tape backing. Just peel and apply along window edges where it will be seen. Take a look at a window with a system installed to see how it's applied, with one end of the wire running off the glass onto the frame. If you can't find the tape, make your own using thin wire and a clear, sturdy tape that won't crack and peel from sunlight. Stretch the wire taut on window surface and apply tape to hold it in place.

• Security system or fake, anybody can enter through an unlocked door. Remember to lock!

THE EYES HAVE IT

What they see is what they get

Some estimates say ninety-five percent of thieves check out a building before breaking in—"case the joint" by looking in windows, trying the doors, and noting valuables.

And the pros know just where to look once they're

> A THIEF WANTS TO ENTER ONLY IF HE
> BELIEVES THERE'S SOMETHING
> WORTH TAKING, AND HE WANTS TO
> GET IN AND OUT AS QUICKLY AS
> POSSIBLE. HE'S NOT LIKELY TO WASTE
> A LOT OF TIME SEARCHING.

inside—the buffet for the silver, the bedroom for jewelry. Most of the time the prize is exactly where they expect it.

You can reduce temptation by limiting what they can see and making the rest hard to find.

SIMPLE THINGS TO DO:

• From outside, look in your windows and move any valuables that are visible. While you're at it, check latches and locks. See #27, Batten Down the Hatches.

• Close drapes and blinds at night and when you're away, including those on the backyard side.

• Think about the valuables in your house. How logical are their locations? Consider moving each to a place out of view and not likely to be searched—under the kitchen sink, in the pantry, under the sofa, in the refrigerator.

• Those wonderful little soda can "safes" really do work, as do phony electrical outlets and other fakes. They're available inexpensively in novelty or hardware stores. Or make your own—any empty can makes a dandy container for cash or small items if it's on a high shelf where you can't see the missing lid. Your entire jewelry collection will fit rolled in a cloth in an empty laundry detergent box. You can improvise a dozen great camouflages on your own.

• At holiday time, the incidence of burglaries goes up. Don't put out presents too soon. Many of us open our drapes to show off a bright Christmas tree; be careful about also showing off your pile of presents.

TWO PLACES AT ONCE

How to be there when you're not

The vast majority of crimes against property occur in homes or businesses where no one is present. It's logical that most thieves would rather simply help themselves to your belongings than have to deal with someone who clearly wishes otherwise.

We all must be away sometimes, but we don't have to leave our possessions completely vulnerable to

A SILENT, EMPTY HOUSE OR BUSINESS
IS A SIGNAL THAT NO ONE IS THERE TO
PROTECT IT. WHEN YOU CAN'T
ACTUALLY BE PRESENT, MAKE THEM
THINK YOU ARE.

crime. It doesn't take a magician to be in two places at once.

SIMPLE THINGS TO DO:

• Inexpensive timers are available for electrical devices. Buy several, and set them evenings for lights and a television in the den, later for the bedroom lamp, etc. Remember to include noise along with light.

• If away for more than a day or two, get forty-eight-hour timers so patterns can vary every other day, or have a friend reset them periodically.

• Use the automatic on-off features on various appliances, such as your television or clock radio, to add a bit of periodic "activity" to your empty rooms.

• Use a simple tape recorder and the longest tape you can find to record average activities around your house. Simply leave it on during dinner, washing dishes, family conversation, or whatever occurs. Then put the tape in your stereo on continuous play while you're out.

• There is no rule saying you can't use outside motion detectors for lights on the inside—it's the same wiring as for outside fixtures, just a longer wire. A light suddenly going on inside as he approaches your house may send a would-be thief running.

• Most of us have a neighbor pick up mail and newspapers when we're away—good practices we should follow every time we leave. If gone for more than a day or two, also ask the neighbor to park a car in the driveway now and then, open curtains here and there during the day, keep lawn mowed and snow shoveled, and put a trash can out on the regular day. Don't use "vacation stops" for newspapers; the fewer people who know you're away the better. It's better to cancel and start service again when you return.

• If your phone company offers call forwarding, use it to have your calls answered by a friend who can take messages. Remind the friend not to tell anyone of your absence.

• If you ever return home, whether gone an hour or a month, to find a door ajar, a window broken, or anything out of order, DO NOT go inside. Go somewhere else and call police immediately.

BATTEN DOWN THE HATCHES

Doors and windows are entry points

Now is the time to take a thorough look at the security of your doors and windows. It's easy to let things go— fix that loose knob later, forget about that key you lost, leave the door unlocked just to dash to a neighbor's.

Most burglars enter in less than sixty seconds. Any-

IN AS MANY AS FIFTY PERCENT OF ALL
BURGLARIES, THE INTRUDER WALKS
RIGHT IN, WITH LITTLE OR NOTHING TO
STOP HIM. IT TAKES VERY LITTLE
EFFORT TO PREVENT THIS
HAPPENING TO YOU.

---

thing you can do to slow them down is good crime prevention. It bears repeating again and again . . .

SIMPLE THINGS TO DO:

• Lock your doors and windows—so simple. Develop the habit, so you do it without thinking. Do it when you come home. Do it when you leave, even for a few minutes. Check it when you go to bed. Be sure the kids do, too.

• Make sure outside doors are 1-3/4" solid core, not hollow. If you live in an apartment building, insist that management install solid entrance doors. If you own your home, do it yourself. Good doors aren't cheap, but they are worth the cost.

• In all outside doors install a dead bolt and reinforce the strikeplate in the frame. For this essential security, your cost can be as low as $25 and less than thirty minutes of your time. Do it now. See #28, Dead Bolt Do's and Don'ts.

• Check windows fasteners also. Many builders use less expensive locks that are easy to break. Excellent secondary locks are available, and a locksmith can advise you about the best types for the style of your windows and the fire codes in your area. Add a device that will also enable you to lock windows when they are opened slightly for ventilation.

• Never nail windows shut for security. You must be able to exit in case of a fire or other emergency.

• Install storm windows.

• For especially vulnerable windows, ask your hardware store about window gates, which bar entry even if glass or screens are broken. Install the kind that open from the inside, and be sure they meet local fire codes.

• Sliding glass doors can have added security by installing a "Charlie bar," available at hardware stores, or by simply cutting a broomstick to length and placing it in the sliding track where it will prevent opening. Two or three screws in the top inside frame with heads protruding slightly will prevent the sliding door from being lifted out.

• Garage doors are entry doors. Treat them as any other outside door, with substantial locks. See also #29, Safety Is the Key.

• Burglars sometimes use small children to gain access through pet doors. Don't install one larger than six or eight inches across. Let larger animals in and out yourself.

DEAD BOLT DOs AND DON'Ts

Improving on a good thing

You've got locks on every door and you probably feel safe with them. The fact is, though, that many of the locks on doors and windows just don't keep intruders

IN MANY HOME BREAK-INS, A DOOR
OR WINDOW IS SIMPLY BATTERED
UNTIL IT GIVES, LOCKS OR NO LOCKS.
THE QUALITY OF YOUR LOCKS AND THE
WAY THEY'RE INSTALLED MAKE A HUGE
DIFFERENCE IN YOUR VULNERABILITY
TO BREAK-INS. CHECK THEM
CAREFULLY.

out. It's well worth your time and a little expense to make this first line of defense as impenetrable as you can.

SIMPLE THINGS TO DO:

• Do this inspection: Check each of the locks on your doors and windows and replace it immediately if it has any of these common problems:

–Is it loose? Does it move when you touch it?

–Is it necessary to jiggle the knob in order to turn or depress the locking button on the inside?

–Do you have to push on or wiggle the key before it will turn in the lock?

–Is it hard to get the key out of the lock?

–Do you have to slam or push up or down on the door for it to close or lock?

• Install dead bolts in every entrance door—locking doorknobs are simply not effective against break-ins. The minimum: hardened steel dead bolts with 1" to 1-1/2" throw and metal strikeplate. A locksmith can show you a variety, costing from $25 up. Get the best you can afford. They're worth every penny.

• Check the screws that hold the strikeplate—the rectangular plate in the door frame where the dead bolt slides in. This is the point of greatest vulnerability to bashing—the screws simply give way. Most manufacturers use inadequate one-inch screws. Simply replace these screws with the longest screws your door frame will handle. Two-, three-, or even four-inch screws may fit. Replacing existing screws is easy. Be sure the new longer screws are the same gauge (thickness) so they fit the strikeplate's holes. Your hardware salesperson can match the gauge—take a screw from your door frame with you to the store.

- If your doors are wood or plastic, also have the salesperson show you the new wraparound metal plates available in most door thicknesses.

- USE your locks. Remember the fifty percent of burglaries that are walk-ins? Get in the habit of locking doors automatically when you're inside, and teach the kids to do the same. See #27, Batten Down the Hatches.

◦ |29| ◦

SAFETY IS THE KEY

It's 10 P.M. Do you know where your keys are?

Is there anyone who doesn't have a drawer, a chain, or a can brimming with mystery keys for which there is no lock, no clue, and no memory?

There's probably not much risk in having a bunch of

> KEYS ARE A CRITICAL PART OF THE
> SECURITY OF YOUR HOME OR
> BUSINESS AND THE PEOPLE IN IT.
> KNOW WHERE THEY ARE AND USE THE
> SAME CARE WITH THEM YOU'D USE
> WITH CASH OR ID.

keys with no locks, but having a lock without all of its keys is another matter altogether.

It's a mistake to be casual about keys. Take time now to be sure they're accounted for and well protected.

SIMPLE THINGS TO DO:

• Take an inventory of all of the keys to locks or equipment you own or use—kids love this job, sorting and counting. If you can't locate all of the keys you should have for a particular lock, rekey it. Learn to do it yourself where you can—it's a ten-minute job with a screwdriver. Cars probably require a locksmith, but it's still cheap insurance.

• If there are several different keys or a lot of people with a legitimate need for your keys, such as in a business, keep a written, up-to-date record of how many keys and who has what.

• There are times when rekeying locks is a must:

—When a worker who was given or had access to keys leaves your employ, at a business or at home.

—When remodeling or other construction work is completed.

—When you change residences. Insist on this from landlords, and do it when you buy a home.

—When a key is missing.

• An electric garage door opener is a key. Treat it like one. Don't leave the control in your car or with papers that bear your address, like car registration or wallet.

• Right now, go get any spare keys you have hidden under doormats, on ledges, under rocks or planters.

Leave a spare with a trusted neighbor, never outside.

• Don't put your name, address, or license number ID on any key ring. Carry your key ring in a separate pocket, not with your wallet or in your purse. Don't carry a spare house or car key in your wallet or anywhere your address appears.

• In parking garages, when valet parking, or when leaving your car for repairs, leave the attendant, valet, or mechanic only the key to your car's ignition, not the entire ring. There are special separating key rings that are handy for anyone who uses such services frequently.

• Computer passwords, electronic security codes, safe combinations, and PIN numbers for credit cards are keys, too. Don't give them out. Don't write them down. If you MUST have a written record, keep it in your safety deposit box only.

⋄|30|⋄

EASY TO BE HARD

Thwarting car thieves with simple habits

Here's a truly amazing fact: forty percent of all cars stolen in the U.S. had the keys in the ignition at the time. Another one: eighty percent were unlocked. Maybe there's a clue here to master the obvious?

It's easy to develop simple habits that don't cost a penny but DO reduce the chances you'll lose your car to a thief. The harder you make it for these criminals, the lower the chances.

CAR THIEVES STEAL THE CARS THAT
ARE EASIEST TO STEAL, SO MAKE
YOURS THE TOUGHEST ON THE BLOCK.

SIMPLE THINGS TO DO:

• Get in the habit of removing keys, rolling up windows tightly, and locking doors every time you leave the car, no matter how brief the errand. A routine that includes all three will reduce the chance of theft enormously.

• When you park in a driveway, park with the back in and the engine facing toward the street. It's easier to see a thief who may try to "hot-wire" or tamper with your car.

• No matter where you park, develop the habit of turning the wheels as far as possible to the right or left before turning off the ignition and engaging the column lock. Some very sophisticated thieves will try to tow a car away—much harder with turned, locked wheels.

• Park as close to a streetlight as possible and on the busiest street possible. Remember that light, noise, and activity are crime's worst enemies.

• When using valet parking, check that the attendant is a real employee (yes, sometimes thieves pose as attendants). Once certain, give him only the car key, not your entire key ring.

• If you must leave your car parked overnight or for a long time, remove the rotor or coil wire to make it impossible to run. It takes only seconds. Ask your mechanic to show you where these are in your vehicle.

• There are mixed reviews about the new "club" type steering wheel locks, but though they are not foolproof, anything that is visible through the window and makes theft more difficult is probably a good idea. Call local police to ask their opinion.

• Car alarms have also been debated, but certainly having one is better than not. Experts say that an alarm won't stop the pros, but amateurs will usually pass up a car with alarm protection.

• Other devices which are helpful include:
  —locking lug bolts on wheels
  —locking gas cap
  —"no knob" inside door lock buttons
  —kits for etching window glass with identification

• Make copies of a slip of paper on which you've written the Vehicle Identification Number (VIN), license number, and description of your vehicle, and serial numbers of stereos, CB radios, etc., which are in your car. Slip one of these copies into the hollow between the window and inside frame of each of the car's doors, under the carpet in the trunk, and other hidden places. While this won't prevent car theft, it can make your car more traceable later.

• Carry your registration and insurance verification on your person, not in your car. You do not want a car thief to also have your address.

• When you are selling a vehicle, don't let a test driver take the car out alone. Sometimes they don't come back! And when buying a vehicle, check the Vehicle Identification Number and other numbers against the paperwork you're given.

• Boat owners, most of the tips above apply to you as well.

SHOW AND STEAL

You don't have to invite trouble

We all know by now that criminals look for opportunity. Leaving something in plain view in an empty car is like ringing the dinner bell—an invitation to come and get it.

The simple precautions that best protect us from

> THE EASIER YOU MAKE IT FOR A THIEF
> TO SEE WHAT'S IN YOUR CAR, THE
> GREATER THE LIKELIHOOD HE WILL TRY
> TO BREAK IN. A CAR THAT APPEARS
> EMPTY LEAVES HIM LITTLE
> TEMPTATION.

car burglary are obvious, but theft happens so frequently that such advice clearly needs to be emphasized. Your best insurance is once again your own routine.

SIMPLE THINGS TO DO:

• A common thief's ploy is to ask for help at your window, then reach in and grab the purse you've put beside you on the seat. While driving, keep your purse, wallet, and checkbook under the seat or in the glove box—somewhere out of sight—and take them with you when you leave the car. See #33, Blind Spots and Bumper Cars.

• Put store purchases, gym bags, the present for a friend, etc., in the trunk before driving to your next destination. Don't leave them inside the car where they can be seen.

• Carry a small blanket or towel in the same color as your car's carpeting. If you absolutely must put parcels where they can be seen, in a van, for example, put them on the floor and cover them with the towel. It's not foolproof, but it may help make items a little less noticeable.

• Even papers, like bills or letters, when left in open view can give thieves useful information that can make you a target in another way—by revealing your address, account numbers, etc.

• Lock stereo tapes, portable antenna, CB radio, and other electronics in the trunk. If it becomes part of your routine, it's not much hassle to plug in the stereo each time you get in, or to put just the two or three tapes you'll be playing this trip in the glove box. Car phones are especially popular among thieves these days and are very difficult to trace.

• Please, please, please don't leave children alone in a parked car for even one second.

OUT AND
ABOUT

❖

Tips for Safer Comings
and Goings

THE CONSCIOUS COMMUTER

Getting there, safe and sound

Nearly all of us leave home daily to travel to work or school. Because we get familiar with the schedules and routes we take, it's easy to become complacent, letting our minds drift during our daily commute. Here are some suggestions to make all that moving about a little safer.

SIMPLE THINGS TO DO:

- Driving: Keep your doors locked, windows rolled up or cracked only slightly. Use your instincts when asked for directions or handed a flyer. When stopping for gas, for a burger, at the ATM, or right in front of the dry cleaners, turn off the ignition and lock up. If you pass a car that appears to be broken down, drive to the nearest phone and call police rather than stop. See #33, Blind Spots and Bumper Cars.
- Carpool. It's safer to be with people than alone.
- Park where it's well lighted and in the clear, away

WE'RE UNAVOIDABLY MORE
VULNERABLE WHEN DRIVING OR
RIDING PUBLIC TRANSPORTATION IN
OUR DAILY ROUTINES, EVEN WHEN
TRAVELING FAMILIAR ROUTES.
DEVELOPING A FEW HABITS FOR
SPECIFIC SITUATIONS WILL GO A LONG
WAY TOWARD INCREASING BOTH
SAFETY AND CONFIDENCE.

from Dumpsters, shrubs, large vans or trucks, or occupied vehicles. Use garages or lots with attendants when you can, and leave only the ignition key, with no identification. In a lot, choose a space near the main traffic flow. In some situations, parking tail-in can make a car theft attempt more visible. Wherever you park, turn wheels very sharply to the left or right to foil attempts at towing. Take a moment to put valuables and ID away—see #31, Show and Steal.

• If you can, get a car phone or CB radio so that in an emergency your call for help is immediate. Don't forget to stash it in the trunk when you park.

• Scan the inside of your car, front and back, BEFORE you get in. And lock the door behind you.

• It can't be said enough. Don't hitchhike and don't pick up hitchhikers.

• At bus and train stops, schedule your arrival to minimize your waiting time.

• Look around BEFORE you get in a bus, taxi, or train. In any situation your best course is to avoid trouble before it happens.

• Sit near the bus driver or conductor. Keep briefcase, purse, or parcels in your lap.

• Most of the tips for making yourself less a target when you're on foot also apply when you're taking public transportation. See #38, Walking Tall.

BLIND SPOTS AND BUMPER CARS

Carjacking and how to avoid it

An estimated 28,000 carjackings occurred in 1992. This particularly vicious form of car theft is a fairly recent invention and is a fast-rising crime in America's cities, occurring often in rush-hour traffic and in broad daylight.

Carjacking is a crime of opportunity, which makes it important and possible to reduce risk by knowing what to watch for and how carjackers work.

SIMPLE THINGS TO DO:

• One inviolable rule: if approached, don't get out of your car. If you're out, do not get in. Ever. Once you are in a car with a stranger, the situation becomes ominous. This is a basic rule for all people and all kinds of crime.

• Check doors to be sure they're locked each time you get in the car. Kids can develop this habit, too, and you can check it with them just as you do when you

> UNLIKE THEFT OF A PARKED VEHICLE,
> CARJACKING TARGETS PEOPLE IN A CAR
> AS WELL AS THE CAR ITSELF, AND
> PERSONAL INJURY IS ALWAYS A
> POSSIBILITY. FOCUS ON ELIMINATING
> OPPORTUNITY AND GETTING FAR AWAY
> FROM POTENTIAL TROUBLE.

ask if seat belts are fastened. That "one-button-locks-all-doors" feature of many new cars is wonderfully useful, so use it if you have it. In slow traffic or at stops, keep windows up or cracked only slightly for ventilation.

• At stops leave at least a car length between you and the car ahead—in the event of trouble, you have the space to drive away.

• Drive in the center lane where it's harder for anyone to approach your car.

• Carjackers often approach in the "blind spot" of your mirror—the same blind spot you learned about in driver training courses in high school. If you must drive frequently in high-risk areas, add an aftermarket mirror that broadens your rear view; there are many to choose from. Remember that a criminal's advantage often lies in the element of surprise. Remove the surprise and you lessen his advantage.

• Another tactic carjackers use is to "bump and rob." If you are bumped from behind, turn on your flashers, memorize the other car's license plate if you can, and drive slowly to a gas station to call for assistance or until you see a police car. If it's an accident, you'll need a report anyway, and if it's not, you'll discourage any ill intentions. Under NO circumstances roll down the window or get out of your car unless you are absolutely sure it's okay.

• If anyone approaches your car for help or for any reason, speak to them only through a slightly cracked window. If they need assistance, drive away and make a call from somewhere else. This includes approaches by people dressed as police but riding in an unmarked car (phony marked cars are rare). Some 235,000 crimes are committed every year by police imposters. Be respectful but cautious until you've verified it's an officer by asking for ID.

• If for any reason you can't drive away from any situation that makes you uncomfortable, lean on your horn, trigger the alarm, draw as much attention as possible to your car. See #34, Simple Signals.

• Keep valuables out of sight. See #31, Show and Steal.

• Carjackers are often vicious. If you are actually carjacked, give up your car. No arguments. But under no circumstances go with them, even if ordered to.

SIMPLE SIGNALS

Some safer ways to holler for help

Sooner or later we all need to rely on the kindness of strangers. Most often it's simply a flat tire or we've lost our way. Occasionally it's because something's really amiss.

Regardless of the reason, your objective is to get assistance on the way quickly and safely.

> AN EMERGENCY IS A TIME WHEN
> TEMPORARILY YOU HAVE LESS
> CONTROL AND LESS ABILITY TO
> RETREAT. PLAN AHEAD TO ASSURE
> YOUR SAFETY AND A FAST
> RESOLUTION.

SIMPLE THINGS TO DO:

• Keep your car well maintained—tire pressure, well tuned, charged, and a spare in good condition—and refill with gas when you reach ¼ tank. Keep emergency flashers and horn in working condition.

• In the event of car trouble or accident, stop and think, assess the situation, use your instincts. If there is any question of safety, stay in the car. In addition to your road emergency kit with jumper cables, flares, and jack, which you carry in the trunk, carry an emergency signal pack INSIDE, under the seat or in the glove box. In it, put:

–A white cloth you can tie on the doorknob that signals you are disabled and need assistance. If in a safe area, get out briefly and raise the hood. Both of these signals are widely recognized.

–A police-type whistle (much louder than the kind coaches use). Consider also an inexpensive "aerosol can" blast horn of the type required by the Coast Guard as safety equipment on boats and sold at marine supply stores.

–Some pieces of poster board on which you've written "CALL POLICE" in very large, thick letters so it can be seen at a distance. Wedge the signs in your windows in an emergency. You can carry a couple of blank pieces and a marking pen also.

–An envelope containing three or four quarters. On the outside, clearly print a list of several phone numbers to call, in order of priority. It's not necessary to include a lot of information, just first name and phone number of your spouse, a relative, a friend, the police or towing company—a brief list of the people you yourself would call if stranded. If someone offers to help, roll down the window an inch or so to hand them the envelope and ask them to make the calls for you. Keep the same kind of envelope in your wallet, in your luggage, and other important places.

• In the event of a serious emergency or if you are isolated or afraid, use your car's horn or your whistle in the universal emergency SOS pattern—three short blasts, three long ones, three short, three long, and so on.

• If involved in a minor accident, motion the other driver to follow you and slowly drive to a public place where you can call police.

• Do not accept rides to the service station. Don't EVER get into a car with a stranger.

• A car phone is an excellent emergency device. Buy one if you can afford it.

• Keeping your cool in the face of other drivers' actions, rude words, or gestures is always a good practice to avoid trouble in the first place.

⬥ |35| ⬥

ON THE ROAD AGAIN

Keep vacations positively memorable

The family's been in the car for hours, glad to break for lunch. At a restaurant along the way you scatter in every direction—to the restrooms, the diner, to see the view of the mountains. Back in the parking lot a curious onlooker spots the brochures on the dash and the suitcase on the floor and can't resist the temptation to see if there's a camera in there somewhere. When you think about it, vacation time is the perfect time for opportunity-alert thieves.

While you can't do anything about your out-of-state license plate, you CAN do a lot to make your car uninteresting to a would-be thief.

SIMPLE THINGS TO DO:

• Keep maps, brochures, tickets, etc., in glove compartment or purse. When you take one out to read it,

> CRIMINALS KNOW THAT VACATIONERS
> CARRY EVERYTHING IN THEIR
> CARS—CASH, CAMERAS, PERSONAL
> ITEMS. "GO NATIVE" TO MAKE
> YOURSELF AND YOUR VALUABLES
> INCONSPICUOUS WHEN TRAVELING
> BY CAR.

unfold it in your lap, not high in the window. Minimize the appearance that you are a traveler.

• Those clothing hooks in the backseat are handy for a jacket but as a traveling closet they're too enticing to window-shoppers. Pack clothing in a suitcase and press it if needed when you get there.

• Once again, master the obvious: camcorders, cameras, wallets, or binoculars sitting in plain view are trouble waiting to happen. Keep valuables out of sight except when you're using them—make it a habit.

• Be aware that December travel, with its carloads of people and presents, is an especially active time for thieves.

• Unload your car completely at motels and park in a well-lit area close to your room, or if that's not possible, close to the office. If pulling a trailer, lock it, of course, and back it in close to a wall or fence where the door cannot be opened.

- If you must park your car or RV some distance away, remove the rotor or coil wire overnight. Anyone can do it in a few seconds—ask your mechanic to show you how.

- For shorter trips, leave telephone, newspaper delivery, and trash pickup in service. If you'll be gone longer, cancel service altogether and start it again when you return; avoid "vacation stops" on services when you can. During any absence have a neighbor take care of messages and your home's "occupied" appearance. See #26, Two Places at Once.

- Leave copies of your driver's license, passport, credit cards, vehicle registration, and itinerary with someone in case of emergency. See #36, Travel Tactics.

TRAVEL TACTICS

When you're a stranger in a strange land

Americans travel more than anybody—seems like it's part of our character. On business, for pleasure, alone or with the family, anytime we're away from home we've got everything we need with us, either in our luggage or on our person. Thieves know it, and most of us who have traveled have at least one "travel adventure" story that includes a pocket picked or a suitcase stolen.

There are times when the airlines part us from our luggage, and times when we stay at the hotel our company selects, but there's still a great deal we can control.

SIMPLE THINGS TO DO:

• On luggage ID use only your initial and last name, and use a business address, not your home. Use a tag

AT AIRPORTS AND TRAIN STATIONS,
HOTELS AND CONVENTION CENTERS
IN UNFAMILIAR CITIES, WE'RE
PARTICULARLY EXPOSED—BOTH OUR
PERSONS AND OUR PROPERTY.
FOLLOW SIMPLE SECURITY PRACTICES
AND AVOID TURNING YOUR
ADVENTURE INTO A DISASTER.

that has a flap over the address, or cover it with tape.

• Leave a detailed itinerary with someone, and include phone numbers where you can be reached. If your travel plans include several destinations or are lengthy, arrange to call someone regularly to check in, and set a time limit after which they will call police if they cannot locate you.

• Before leaving, call police in your destination city to ask about your hotel. Police know exactly what neighborhoods and which hotels are safe.

• Call the hotel itself to ask about the most direct route from the airport. Use the information to appear more knowledgeable when you speak to cab drivers and others. For example: "Mr. Smith, take me to the Alexander Hotel downtown. It's about five blocks north on Madison from the interstate.'' Use the cab rules in #37, On the Town.

• Travel with as little luggage as possible, even if you plan to check it. Heavily burdened travelers are vulnerable. A good criterion is ''No more than you can easily take inside a public restroom stall.'' Leave your Rolex and camel hair coat at home or, at the very least, packed in a carry-on where they won't be seen.

• If you rent a car, arrange it from home and rent a common vehicle that does not draw attention. For some reason, red cars are targets most frequently, so choose another color.

• Lock your luggage. There are some clever electronic alarms sold in travel stores that trigger on motion; you can use them not only on luggage while it sits in a hotel room but also on the hotel door.

• Use traveler's checks in small denominations, and bring only the credit cards you'll need. Make a photocopy of your passport, driver's license, credit cards, etc., and carry it in a separate place; in case of loss, you'll know exactly what's missing and can easily report it.

• Criminals who work airports and train stations are often experienced and clever and often work in teams of both men and women. Be alert to attempts to distract you or people who move inside your ''personal space.'' Know common tactics used by street criminals. See #38, Walking Tall.

• Make or buy short buckled straps for each suitcase or bag—something the length of a dog collar will do. In waiting rooms or on a long train ride where you could fall asleep or be distracted while your luggage sits next to you, strap each bag handle to the seat leg. You'll be jostled if anyone picks it up.

• Use an inexpensive cloth money pouch, available at travel stores. Each of several styles fits under clothing and is a more secure way to carry important papers, traveler's checks, etc.

• Here's a checklist for picking a hotel room:

–Room doors open to an inside hall, and inside hall has a minimum of entrance/exits, each with passkey access.

–Residential security guard in hotel.

–Reasonable amount of activity in the hall—other guests, hotel personnel.

–All areas of hotel well lit, inside and out.

–Ask for a room close to the desk or an active area of the hotel. Look at the room before you accept it, noting the route and the access as well as the room itself. Watch for burned-out lightbulbs, damage, or any sign that maintenance is poor.

–Have a bellhop accompany you to your room.

• Any of these should send you to another hotel:

–Super-budget hotels or any that fail the tests above.

–No phone in the room.

–Loiterers, a lot of foot traffic, or anyone who looks out of place.

–Convenience or liquor stores very close by.

–Room doors that open to the outside.

–Rooms without solid doors or deadlocking bolts.

• When you leave your hotel, give the front desk an envelope containing a list of contact phone numbers, your itinerary, your description, your vehicle's description, a photocopy of your ID and credit cards. On the outside, print your expected time of return, and instruct the desk to open it and call police if you don't come back. Pick it up when you return, or call the desk if you're running late. Don't feel silly for covering yourself in this way. Time counts more than anything else in an emergency.

◇ |37| ◇

ON THE TOWN

Safer ways to enjoy your leisure time

All of us like a little recreation, to take ourselves to dinner, to the movies or shopping, to the park or beach. When we're having the most fun, it's also easy to pay the least attention—pleasure is an enormous distraction.

Let's all be sure the fun times remain just that!

SIMPLE THINGS TO DO:

• On public transportation—buses, subways, etc.— plan your route in advance and let someone know it. Plan to arrive at your stop shortly before boarding to minimize time standing around—if early, go into a nearby store for the extra few minutes. Once aboard, sit near the driver and away from the exit door. Keep your belongings on your lap, not on the seat or floor.

> THE PLEASURE WE DERIVE FROM
> LEISURE ACTIVITIES IS THE VERY
> FEELING THAT CAN LULL US INTO
> FORGETFULNESS. MAKE SAFETY
> HABITS A MATTER OF COURSE WHEN
> YOU'LL BE OUT AND ABOUT. KNOWING
> YOU'RE PREPARED LEAVES YOU FREE
> TO FULLY ENJOY.

Keep your children in sight, and don't announce your travel plans in casual conversation with strangers.

• Stick to cabs associated with a company and avoid the "bootleg" independents. Make a mental note of the driver's name, which should be in plain view from your seat, and use it when you speak: "Mr. Jones, take me to Dino's Restaurant at Fifth and Broad."

• If driving yourself, use the basic rules of locking doors and keeping windows closed. Park where there's lighting and, if possible, security, and follow basic smart parking rules. See #32, The Conscious Commuter.

• When dropped off by a friend, ask that they wait until you're safely inside.

• At a park or beach, note where an office, a ranger,

or a lifeguard can be found, and picnic or play nearby. Leave valuables in the trunk of your car, and remember where you parked so you're not wandering around later with that recognizable "lost" look.

• Use public restrooms in pairs.

• Carry only the cash and credit cards you need. Your criterion: Is it no big deal if I lose it? Consider a "traveler's wallet," which straps or hangs under your clothing, or a second slim wallet or compact to carry concealed, with spare cash, spare key, etc.

• Give your tip to the server at a restaurant rather than leaving it on the table. Pay attention to your credit cards and receipts when you pay. See #10, The Credit Crunch.

WALKING TALL

Attitude is everything on the street

To a large extent, your outward appearance can influence your chances of being picked as a criminal's next target. Just as the way you dress, the way you speak and carry yourself convey a message to a prospective

MAKE YOURSELF THE LEAST
DESIRABLE TARGET ON THE
STREET—BY DRESSING, WALKING,
CARRYING PARCELS, AND OBSERVING
YOUR SURROUNDINGS WITH PURPOSE
AND CONFIDENCE.

employer or your date for the evening, the same things can say "I'm vulnerable" OR "I'm in control" to a criminal looking to rip you off.

SIMPLE THINGS TO DO:

• Here's a good exercise for everybody, kids included. At the mall or downtown, find a bench and just watch people for a while. You'll quickly see who exudes confidence and who appears vulnerable. Talk together about what makes a person seem weak or strong.

• When you can, walk with a partner or group, whether walking from the subway to work or out for your daily exercise routine. Your dog can be a powerful deterrent, too, and will benefit as much as you from a stroll.

• Do not walk or jog with earphones. Your sense of hearing is important when you're out in public; don't cut it off.

• Wear clothing that allows for freedom of movement—not too tight or too loose. If on business, wear athletic shoes on the street and change to dress shoes at work.

• Dress modestly, leaving the expensive cashmere coat for another time. Same with jewelry—put it on when you get there. Saying "I have money" is downright foolish.

• Make brief, pleasantly neutral eye contact with people on the street. It sends a message of confidence: "I'm aware of you, too." Eye contact is hard for some people, so start first with people you know, then practice in public until it's comfortable. It's an important thing to learn.

• Limit what you carry and try to keep one hand free. If you're making purchases, arrange for delivery of anything heavy or bulky. If you carry any kind of self-defense device, keep it in your hand; it will do you no good in your pocket. See #39, It's in Your Hands. At night carry a flashlight.

• Walk down a clear center part of the sidewalk, even in the street if necessary and possible. Walk wide around corners, past doorways, Dumpsters, and shrubbery, and several feet in from parked cars along the curb.

• Street thieves sometimes bump, shove, cause a commotion, spill drinks, or otherwise jostle a victim, and they sometimes work in teams. Be alert to such distractions.

• Carry your purse or bag close to your body, like a football. The long strap on some purses should cross your body, shoulder to opposite hip. Men, carry wallets in a front pocket. Carry keys separately from your purse or wallet; keys plus ID equals an invitation to a home burglary.

• Wait for the next elevator car rather than entering if only one person is inside or if anything at all feels "off." In an elevator, stand near the control panel where you can punch the button for the next floor or the emergency call if necessary.

• Vary routes for trips you make often, especially for daily tasks such as bank deposits. Be sure someone knows today's route and when you're expected, then stick to your plan. Avoid shortcuts. (Remember that your kids, on the other hand, have a separate set of rules. See #15, Way to Go.)

• If you suspect you are being followed, get to a public place immediately and call police. DO NOT go home.

IT'S IN YOUR HANDS

Gizmos and gadgets to carry with you

More and more of us are carrying small devices—chemical sprays or loud alarms—to protect ourselves when walking or jogging alone.

Law enforcement experts differ in their attitudes

> WHEN ACCOSTED BY SOMEONE WHO
> INTENDS TO HARM OR ROB YOU, YOU
> HAVE NO TIME WHATSOEVER TO PULL
> ANYTHING FROM YOUR POCKET. IF
> YOU CARRY ANY KIND OF PROTECTIVE
> DEVICE, CARRY IT IN YOUR HAND.

toward these devices, but they do agree on one thing: a spray or alarm tucked in a purse or pocket is as good as nothing at all.

SIMPLE THINGS TO DO:

• The disabling sprays that are legal in your area are carried at hardware stores, security stores, and sometimes at large discount stores. Look at a variety of styles, sizes, and chemical types.

• Sprays come in several sizes, from a 6- or 7-inch-tall canister in a holster, often carried by police, to very tiny, lipstick-size canisters for a single use. Whichever you choose, carry it in your hand while on the street and return it to purse or pocket only when you arrive.

• The same goes for sound alarms. You won't have time to grab for one, so carry it. They operate very much like the sprays, with a button to push, and many are small enough to fit in a closed fist.

• An alternative if you don't own a special device is your own keys. It's a good idea to have keys in your hand before you reach your car anyway, so that you're not standing at the car door fumbling in purse or pocket to find them. Whenever you're walking, hold your key ring in your closed palm with two or three keys protruding between your fingers. A hard punch in the face with those sharp points will be a painful message to anyone who makes a threatening move.

• Other good improvised weapons include pen or pencil, comb with a rat-tail end, a heavy flashlight, umbrellas. The best force is an overhand downward motion. See #42, If the Worst Happens.

SHOP TALK

Ways to avoid buying trouble

Going downtown, to the supermarket, or to the mall for a day of shopping is a regular event for most of us. It's a time when we relax and enjoy, but also a time when we often become tired, burden ourselves with boxes and bags, get distracted by noise, activity, the dinner menu, or our own cranky kids.

SHOPPING, WITH ITS CROWDS AND

CONFUSION, CAN MAKE US ESPECIALLY

VULNERABLE TO THIEVES. BE SAFER

BY KNOWING WHAT THEY'RE LOOKING

FOR, KNOWING WHAT TO DO, AND

PLANNING AHEAD.

Take a few special precautions and think ahead. It can save you more than just money on a shopping trip.

SIMPLE THINGS TO DO:

• Mall or store restrooms are usually located far away from activity. Consider stopping somewhere else to use the restroom before you arrive at the store. When you do use a mall restroom, go in pairs. Never, ever allow a child to go into any public restroom alone. Take them in with you—either gender—until they are mature enough to handle a crisis alone.

• As always when in a public place, carry only the amount of cash you'll need, the credit cards you'll need, the identification you'll need. Don't use cash for large purchases. Keep your wallet or purse with you on your person, not in a shopping cart, in the dressing room, or on the restroom floor.

• If you're doing a lot of shopping, plan your store stops to begin with the cheapest and end with the most expensive purchases. Make trips to the car to put purchases in the trunk before you begin to get loaded down with bags and boxes. If you're concerned about a thief watching, load your trunk and then move your car to another parking place. In any case, avoid becoming vulnerable to personal attack by carrying too much.

• If purchasing bulky items, arrange to have them delivered rather than carrying them to the car yourself.

• While you're arranging for delivery, writing a check, or filling out a refund slip, don't recite your address or phone number where it can be overheard by a casual listener. Rather, if the information is required, get the form from the clerk and write it yourself.

• Be aware of personal information you give away in casual conversation. ''This shirt will be perfect for our cruise next week!'' may say far more than is wise to reveal.

• Have car keys in hand before you leave the store so you aren't fumbling for them at the car door.

• Be thinking, not daydreaming, as you approach your car, and note anyone nearby, in or out of a vehicle. Loading an open car makes it more vulnerable to car thieves AND makes your children vulnerable if they're inside. Leave your baby strapped in the shopping cart seat while you load groceries or purchases, and ask older children to wait before they get in. When fully loaded and before putting keys in the ignition, have older children climb in, lock their doors, and buckle up as you do the same, and strap baby in for a safe drive home.

WORKING ASSETS

Special considerations for the workplace

In the nineties we can't discuss crime, it seems, without specific attention to what we've come to know as "crime in the workplace."

Crime costs U.S. businesses an estimated $100 billion each year in direct losses, legal expenses, and se-

---

LOSSES FROM WORKPLACE CRIME CAN
PUT A COMPANY OUT OF BUSINESS. BY
PREVENTING CRIME AT WORK YOU'RE
NOT JUST PROTECTING THE COMPANY,
YOU'RE PROTECTING YOUR JOB.

---

curity. Most vulnerable are smaller businesses, not giant corporations.

It's a common misconception that crime against business comes from outside the company. In fact, MOST business crime is done by employees. While it's beyond our scope here to discuss white-collar crime, computer crime, industrial espionage, or the like, those of us who go to work each day can and should take precautions at the shop, factory, or office to prevent crimes that have become common in the working world. And, most of the other tips in this book apply at work as well as in our private lives.

SIMPLE THINGS TO DO:

• In most businesses there's a constant stream of people in and out—customers, delivery people, employees, salespeople. Use strict guidelines for allowing anyone unfamiliar past the front counter or desk. See #7, Your Open-Door Policy. A good policy is to have an employee escort all visitors.

• Keep doors and windows locked during business hours. Make public entrances that must remain unlocked as visible as possible, both from the street and by employees inside.

• Theft thrives in anonymity. Greet all of the people who enter your area, either verbally or with a nod. Be aware of bulky coats, bags, parcels, umbrellas, etc., where objects could be hidden by visitors or by employees leaving the building.

• Retail employees should be trained and practiced in making positive identification for checks and credit cards and in recognizing counterfeit money. Check with your local Small Business Administration office and with the FBI for information.

• Burglaries and robberies account for about $12 billion each year in losses, mostly from businesses that are unprotected by electronic alarms. Install one if you can, and test it frequently.

• At night, leave lights on inside your office, workshop, or store. Install inside lights around the cash register and leave the register drawer wide open to show a potential burglar there's nothing there.

• Businesses that are largely cash retail, are in a high crime area, or have many negotiable instruments on hand during the day should make frequent deposits to minimize the amount in the register or safe. Post notices conspicuously announcing the fact that there's not a lot of cash in the building. If it's impossible to make several deposits each day, a well-concealed safe or hidden locked drawer is a possible alternative.

• Robbers look for the predictable. When making your deposits, whether several times a day or at the end of each day, vary your pattern, including the door you leave by, the bag or briefcase you carry, the vehicle you use, and your route to the bank. Your parking place, always in the open and visible, should also vary, and you may be able to use different bank branches. Each time be sure someone knows the route you're taking and set a time to be back or check in. See #38, Walking Tall.

• In your cash drawer keep a small stack of bills that can serve as evidence if ever you are robbed or burgled in spite of all precautions. Don't mix these bills with the bills you use to make change, but do keep a record of their denominations, series, and serial numbers. Your record can be used by police to trace the robber.

• Keep honest people honest by removing temptation. During the workday, place your wallet or purse and other valuables in a locked drawer or other secured place. If you hang your jacket on your chair back or coat rack, remove your wallet from the pocket. Leave expensive jewelry or gadgets at home. Employers, provide lockers or other security for valuables.

• Theft of information has become an enormous problem in the business world. Know and follow your company's security and safety procedures. Be careful of leaving desks with proprietary information in plain view, on a running computer, or in a laptop, which itself could be stolen.

• The federal government offers a number of pamphlets and books on safeguarding particular businesses from various kinds of crime. Contact the U.S. Government Bookstore or a Small Business Administration office, both found in most large cities, or write for a catalog (mention the topics you're interested in) from the Government Printing Office, Superintendent of Documents, Washington, DC 20402.

OUR GREATEST
FEARS

❖

Tips to Consider When
All Else Fails

IF THE WORST HAPPENS

Plan ahead and keep the odds on your side

This book is full of ways to help you stop crime from happening in the first place, and that's what we all want, of course. However, there isn't a single one of us who hasn't had the chilling realization that regardless

> KNOWING AHEAD OF TIME WHAT YOU'LL DO IF THREATENED OR ASSAULTED IS ONE OF YOUR MOST POWERFUL DEFENSIVE WEAPONS. KEEP THE ELEMENT OF SURPRISE ON YOUR SIDE. PLAN AND REHEARSE FOR SAFETY.

of what we do, we can't make any situation 100% certain against the possibility of assault.

A criminal has a plan, and probably a backup plan as well. You should, too. There is no hard and fast rule for what to do if grabbed or threatened, and this book doesn't presume to train you in self-defense, but thinking through unpleasant possibilities and planning what you will do in each of those circumstances will go far toward tipping the odds in your favor if an assault occurs.

SIMPLE THINGS TO DO:

• Identify situations in your life where you could be vulnerable in spite of all precautions. Make up scenarios that could really occur, based on routes you typically take, things you typically do. Imagine the place, the time of day, the sounds, the smells, and imagine what could actually happen. Uncomfortable as it is, go into detail—waking at the sound of an intruder in your bedroom, being surprised from behind on your daily jog or robbed at gunpoint in your store, the feeling of your heart pounding right out of your chest, your parched throat, and sweating palms.

• There is no single answer that can tell you what to do in a particular circumstance—you must depend on your own judgment, as well as on your disposition and training. But if you have mentally rehearsed some frightening scenarios AND some possible responses, you will be in a much stronger position. Decide on a plan for each of your scenarios and rehearse them again and again in your mind. Your objective, remember, is to have some familiarity with the possibilities so that if the time ever comes, your response does not require on-the-spot planning AND you do not react reflexively in a way that endangers you more. The following suggestions have been offered by experts as possible responses to threatening situations.

• First and always, use your instincts to assess the situation. See #18, Belly Buttons.

• Avoid, retreat, escape—always your first choices.

• As we've said, a criminal can look like anybody. When sizing up a situation or a person you've noticed, ask yourself, "Does s/he belong here? Does that activity seem or 'feel' peculiar?" Whether or not he "looks like a criminal" should never be a consideration.

• Don't let anger win out over fear. Without thinking, you can turn a threatening situation lethal with a sudden outburst or rash defensive action. Stay calm, no matter what it takes.

• Many experts believe that your best course of action if you awaken to the sound of an intruder is to pretend to stay asleep—even though your heart is racing. By far the greatest likelihood is that he is a burglar and wants you to stay asleep. He has a plan in case you awaken, and a confrontation could escalate the situation dangerously. Use the time to plan what you will do if he does not go away.

• If accosted, do something unexpected. See #43, What They Least Expect.

• Use your brain to stall for time to look for an escape route—by asking for a cigarette to "calm your nerves," by dropping to your knees to pray out loud—any way you can think of. If you are threatened with sexual attack, the deadly disease argument may work:

"Do this if you're going to, but I'm HIV positive, and by telling you right now I've met my legal obligation if you get AIDS."

• Get attention. Scream (see #16, You Scream and I Scream), yell, whistle (see #39, It's in Your Hands). You're better off to yell a request than to simply yell "help" in many situations—onlookers freeze when they don't know what to do. Sadly, people often interpret a scuffle between a man and a woman as a domestic matter and ignore it. If this is the situation, yell "Call 911!! I don't know this man!!" whether you do or not.

• There is disagreement among experts on the issue of whether to fight—it's both a situational AND a personal decision, and no one can decide it for you. Reading these suggestions or even a dozen of the many excellent full-length books on self-defense will not make you prepared for the real thing. If you regularly face situations that could put you at risk for your personal safety and decide that an active, fighting defense is what you want to do OR if you decide to own a weapon of any kind, get expert training—not a four-week course at a city college, but serious ongoing training. And practice often—not just the use of the method or weapon but the mental preparation and rehearsal that make it an effective option.

• We occasionally hear stories of remarkable heroism by private citizens, but we don't hear the stories, far more frequent, of what happens when it goes the other way. Remember that there is no such thing as a fate worse than death—no injury, no violation, no humiliation.

WHAT THEY LEAST EXPECT

Elements of surprise . . . and safety

The last thing you want to hear is your husband or wife bursting through the door with the horrifying news, "I just got mugged!!" Or worse, that they were hurt in the process. So together you've taken prudent precautions. You're walking tall—aware and confident. You've already substantially reduced your chances of being a target. The next step is to understand where your advantage lies when all precautions fail.

> THE ELEMENT OF SURPRISE WORKS
> ON THE SIDE OF WHOEVER HAS IT. IN
> YOUR WELL-REHEARSED PLANS,
> INCLUDE THE UNEXPECTED.

You know it's important to mentally rehearse situations that could really occur, and you know that having surprise on his side is a great advantage to a thief or mugger. He knows before you do what's going to happen, and he's thought about what he'll do if you fight or scream. You may turn the advantage your way by doing the last thing he'd ever expect.

SIMPLE THINGS TO DO:

• Remember, there is no hard and fast rule to cover every situation. Fear can be paralyzing, so your best strategy is to have already planned and mentally rehearsed your responses to a variety of possibilities until each is familiar. Having a plan will make you calmer and keep your brain working rationally. See #42, If the Worst Happens.

• A mugger or thief has a set of expectations of his victim—resistance, crying, a scream. Include in your plan something so completely ridiculous he cannot have considered it ahead of time—cluck like a chicken or quack like a duck. Some more possibilities:

• One police detective suggests pretending you are going to vomit—lean over, gag, and retch. If you can stick your finger down your throat and actually vomit, so much the better. Urinating or defecating are possibilities, too. Make yourself utterly repulsive. Facing a target whose bodily functions are out of control is probably a situation for which a potential attacker has no backup plan.

• D-ter and similar products are sold in "spy shops" and other stores where self-defense products are available. It's a tiny vial, carried in a pocket, which when broken emits the most disgusting odor imaginable—so bad it's impossible to describe. A potential victim who is vomiting and stinks to high heaven may seem a very uninteresting target for attack. Be aware, though, that reaching into your pocket may be impossible. See #39, It's in Your Hands.

• Pass out—do it convincingly, falling in a limp heap. This may be most applicable if accosted in a public space where he is not likely to pick you up and carry you. Toss your keys under the car or into the gutter on your way down. If he goes for the keys, that may be your opportunity to run.

• Here's another tip from a police detective: Buy an inexpensive money clip and in it fold a five- or ten-dollar bill around two or more ones. If a thief stops you and demands money, slowly pull the clip out of your pocket or purse, so he will see the bills, and THROW it to the side, as far as you can. Then RUN, yelling at the top of your lungs, in the OPPOSITE direction. If you were a thief, would you follow your noisy target to get more, or would you go to the safe, quiet money lying a few feet away on the ground?

• Whatever you choose, your plan should include staying calm, moving slowly, and keeping aware of your surroundings.

• Remember that no wallet, no jewelry, no car is worth taking personal risk. Surrender property willingly—do not let anger win out over your plan.

• Never, never, never get into a car under any circumstances—by doing so you surrender ALL control. If you find yourself in a car with someone threatening, get out. This is one of the few times it may be less risky to fight now than to find yourself later in the woods alone with an abductor.

• If followed on foot, change direction, cross the street, show him you are suspicious by turning around and looking behind you. Walk immediately to a lighted store or house and call the police. DO NOT walk home.

• If a situation warrants, yell "Call the police!!" rather than "help." If you are a woman, also yell, "I don't know this man!!" even if you do. In this country, observers of a scuffle between a man and a woman sometimes interpret it as "merely" a domestic matter and fail to take it seriously. See #44, Home, Violent Home.

• Learn to ignore discourtesies. Dirty looks, rude gestures, getting cut off, interrupted, even insulted, will not harm you. Responding in kind could. This sort of incident can escalate dangerously. It's not worth it.

• The best protection against street crime is to walk in well-lit, well-patrolled, well-traveled areas. If you don't know the neighborhood, take a cab.

• Purses, packs, wallets, and jewelry are a thief's objectives. Make them hard to get when on the street— carry your purse with its strap across your body, your wallet in a different place than your purse or usual pocket, your money in a different place than your wallet, your watch on the other wrist. You get the picture.

HOME, VIOLENT HOME

A crime by any other name . . .

There's far more to be said about domestic violence than can begin to be covered in a book like this one. It belongs here, though, because it is a crime of terrible violence that touches every one of us and will continue, rampant, until we all—you, your friends, your fam-

> AN ASSAULT, A RAPE, OR A MURDER IS
> A VICIOUS, VIOLENT CRIME NO MATTER
> WHO IS THE VICTIM OR WHO IS THE
> PERPETRATOR. REFUSE TO TOLERATE
> ANY ATTITUDE THAT VIEWS IT
> OTHERWISE.

ily—demand of ourselves and our institutions that it be
treated as the serious crime it is.

If you're tempted to dismiss domestic violence as
something less than criminal, ponder the facts: At least
one quarter of all the murders in the U.S. every year
take place within the family. Every fifteen minutes an
American woman is killed by someone who "loves"
her. Every ten seconds one is beaten. Twenty to fifty
percent of American couples report violence as a regular occurrence in their homes. The single greatest cause
of emergency room treatment for women is domestic
abuse. Battering during pregnancy is the number one
cause of infant deaths and birth defects. Half of all police calls are for domestic violence. During the same
period that 58,000 U.S. soldiers were killed in Viet-
nam, 53,000 U.S. women were murdered by their hus-
bands or boyfriends.

SIMPLE THINGS TO DO:

• Find out more about this crime—there are too few
who have bothered to learn. Call your local domestic
violence hotline, usually listed in the phone book under
community services. Rape crisis centers, district attor-
neys' offices, and health clinics may be able to provide
information also.

• Ninety-five percent of cases are women abused by
their male partners, but be aware that men, children,
gays and lesbians, people of all races and economic
circumstances, are victims of domestic violence. It can
happen to anyone.

• Do not tolerate dismissiveness, jokes, or clichés

about victims of domestic abuse. Speak up when you hear someone speak of domestic violence as not a "real" crime: "He just slapped her a couple of times" or "I'll just have to knock you around—ha ha." If an act is a crime when a stranger does it, it's a crime when it happens at home.

• In this country we punish victims by holding them responsible for their own abuse, by asking why she didn't leave, by assuming the victim "caused" an attack. When you hear of a case of domestic violence, ask instead what is the matter with the ABUSER. Demand that the focus and the blame be placed where they belong.

• Teach girls that there is NEVER justification for allowing themselves to be hit, shoved, slapped, threatened, demeaned, or controlled. Teach boys that neither violence nor control of others is manly, and don't call a boy "a girl" for behavior you consider weak or beneath him.

• Actively support victims of abuse. See #48, Stand by Me.

• If you know of or suspect domestic abuse, or if it is happening to you, call for help immediately. It is not an exaggeration to say it is a matter of life and death, even if you believe the situation is not serious. Your local hotline is a good place to start, or call your state's domestic violence hotline, the National Victim Center at 1-703-276-2880 or 1-800-627-6872, or the National Coalition against Domestic Violence at 1-303-839-1852.

IT'S NOT ABOUT SEX

Know the truth about rape

In spite of increased attention to this life-shattering crime in recent years, too many of us still function under a set of mistaken beliefs about what rape is, who commits it, and who are the victims of it.

Some studies show that as many as one in four

> RAPE IS A CRIME OF CONTROL,
> VIOLENCE, AND HOSTILITY. A RAPIST
> DOES NOT RAPE FOR SEX ANY MORE
> THAN AN ALCOHOLIC DRINKS FOR
> THIRST, AND NO RAPE VICTIM EVER
> WANTED IT TO HAPPEN.

women will be raped at some time. Of those, only seven to ten percent are willing to report the crime at all, according to FBI data. In spite of better laws, that's about one and a quarter million rapes each year which go unreported and unpunished, often because of a victim's well-founded belief that she will herself be blamed or that her rapist will only go free, so why bother. Of those rapes that are reported, about a third result in arrests and far fewer still in convictions.

Clearly, there's a problem with attitudes that allow rape to continue. The situation will change when our attitudes change.

SIMPLE THINGS TO DO:

• Rape is an attempt to control and degrade someone. Refuse to tolerate attitudes or practices that are hostile and domineering to women or place unrealistic expectations on them. Acknowledge men who have examined and reshaped biases they may have learned as boys.

• Demand of the justice system—police, prosecutors, elected officials—that rape be treated seriously and punished severely. Pressure lawmakers to strengthen rape laws.

• Understand that rape is most often committed by someone the victim knows, not by a stranger. "Date" rape and "acquaintance" rape are just two more ways to say it. Rape is rape, whoever commits the crime and whatever the circumstance.

• Rape happens to all kinds of people—very old and very young, rich and poor, and also to boys and men.

And rapists can be anyone—aggressive or shy, attractive or homely, family, friend, or total stranger.

• Teach girls and boys to make a BIG scene if someone touches them in a way they don't like. Teach girls to recognize the feeling that someone is becoming too familiar and to stop at any point she becomes uncomfortable or changes her mind, even if petting is already underway. She is the ONLY person who may decide whether she will have sex, and she does not owe it under any circumstances. If she is pressured physically OR verbally, she should get away. Teach boys that a spoken "yes"—not an implied yes, not an assumed yes, not a "she didn't try to stop me" yes—is the only possible permission for sex. He is fully able to control his actions just as he can refuse a meal even if he is very hungry.

• Act in support of rape victims. Support her decision to file charges and testify. Accompany her to appointments and court. Listen if she wants to talk or let her be silent if she wishes. See #48, Stand by Me.

• If you are at particular risk—a student, actively dating several people, go often to singles hangouts, live alone—find out everything you can about rape from crisis centers, crime prevention organizations, or school counselors. Avoid alcohol or anything that will cloud your judgment, stick with a group, and develop basic prudent crime-prevention habits at home and when out.

REAL
COMMUNITY

❖

Tips for Creating
Permanent Solutions

KNOW YOUR NEIGHBOR

Community is the best security system

Police are quick to note that visible evidence of residents who care—who watch out for one another, who know what's "normal" at the Joneses' or tend to the

IT STARTS SIMPLY, JUST BY OPENING
THE DOOR. GATHER FRIENDS AND
NEIGHBORS TOGETHER NOW AND
BEGIN AN ONGOING DIALOGUE ABOUT
THE PROBLEMS, THE RESOURCES,
AND THE SOLUTIONS
FOR YOUR COMMUNITY.

mail and interior lights for the Smiths while they're away—is the one factor that reduces crime rates in every neighborhood where it exists.

The problem, of course, is that the busy lives we lead, centered on our working lives and nuclear families, seem to get in the way of good, old-fashioned community. If you're concerned about crime in your own neighborhood, here's a way to start to change it, right now, for the better. It helps every time.

SIMPLE THINGS TO DO:

• Invite the people on your block or in your building to gather at your house or in a community room. Include everyone, and tell them what you know: neighborhoods where people know one another, even casually, are safer. So let's get acquainted and talk about common concerns.

• You can open dialogue any way you choose, but encourage people to express their concerns, even if it seems like an endless litany of complaints and frustrations. Understand that it is the things the neighborhood sees as its problems that will motivate people, not what agencies or outsiders claim. It's important to allow people to SAY what they're feeling.

• It's also important to set aside differences. There is a truth well recognized by sociologists: Bias and stereotypes can only be maintained at a distance; the closer we come to a group or individual, the more impossible prejudice becomes. You're gathering to discover what you share in common.

• Begin with simple goals at your first gatherings—to get acquainted and to establish a friendly basis for developing a sense of "the neighborhood." You can compile a list of phone numbers and arrange to make copies to distribute. Agree to increase your general alertness and to call one another if anything seems amiss.

• Before you leave, set a date for another gathering, perhaps at a different home. Someone can volunteer to call everyone on the list as a reminder.

• Broaden your outreach. Here's how to begin to get the larger community involved:

—Write for information on community action and from NCPC and other agencies. Ask police, your district attorney, and your city council for information. See #4, Ask McGruff.

—Find a place to meet. If you expect a couple dozen or more, ask a local church, community hall, or restaurant; most will be happy to be a part of things. Be sure to include local business owners.

—Make a simple flyer, something like, "Join your friends and neighbors to talk about crime in our neighborhood and what we can do about it. Saturday noon, Community Hall. THIS IS IMPORTANT! PLEASE COME." It's meaningful to include that last line that TELLS people to come.

—Make copies and get the word out—on store windows, school and church bulletin boards, mailboxes. This is a good job for enthusiastic kids.

—Just as at your neighbors' gathering, get people to talk about the problems they see. If your group is larger, it helps to use a large tablet to jot things down as they are named. When the list gets pretty full, see if together you can condense it into a few specific areas of concern, and analyze the problems to find some common denominators—young people with nothing to do, for example, or blocks that are poorly lit from dusk to dawn.

–Leaving the problems aside, ask people to brainstorm a list of resources—people and things—you have available in the neighborhood. Certainly "official" resources like police and schools will be mentioned, but also encourage people to begin thinking creatively. Most neighborhoods have retired people, maybe an empty storefront or other space, or local clubs with expertise on an important issue.

–Finally, brainstorm solutions. What can you do, with what you've got right now, to begin to address the problems you see as a community? Some examples: Use this book and materials from the National Crime Prevention Council to learn what to watch for and for more on topics like Operation ID or reinforcing locks (buying items in bulk at a discount might be strong motivation for some!). Discuss what public agencies or government officials can do about specific issues and agree to write letters; real change can happen if enough citizens speak up. Get kids interested in taking an inventory of the neighborhood's problem spots.

• All of this brainstorming will overlap, and things may even seem a little chaotic, but it's almost GUARANTEED you will wind up with a group of people who see possibilities, who are enthusiastic, and who will give of themselves in some way toward the common good. The important thing is to start.

NOT IN MY BACKYARD

How to tell the world your neighborhood cares

Appearances matter, and in the neighborhood, the way things look can matter a great deal when it comes to crime.

A neighborhood speaks loudly for itself to anyone who sees it—whether it says by its graffiti, its refuse,

---

THE WAY YOUR NEIGHBORHOOD
LOOKS DIRECTLY AFFECTS THE WAY
CRIMINALS SIZE IT UP FOR CRIME.
MAKE YOURS SAY "WE CARE" AND
YOU'LL MAKE IT SAFER.

---

and its buildings in disrepair that nobody cares, or whether by its fresh paint and happy bustle that this is an area where people take pride, where neighbors are friends, where someone is watching what happens on its streets. If you were a thief, a drug dealer, or a thug, which neighborhood would you choose?

SIMPLE THINGS TO DO:

• The first step is one you and your neighbors can do together and it's absolutely free. Walk your own building, your streets, your parks, your business district together, noting broken streetlights, abandoned vehicles, graffiti, trash buildup, cracked sidewalks, etc. Then pressure your public works department or property owners to make repairs, add lighting to dark areas, plant greenery, etc. Think about getting the city's co-operation to block off streets where crime is a problem—eliminating escape routes has proven effective where it's been tried.

• Many improvements you can do yourselves on a single Saturday. Paint over graffiti, clean up trash, help small business owners to spruce up their storefronts. Establish a weekly volunteer patrol—how about teenagers?—to spot problems on behalf of the neighborhood.

• Get a group of volunteers to map your neighborhood, marking police and fire stations and local businesses where a neighbor in trouble can rely on help, etc. Kids, help with this. You know more about walking the neighborhood than adults ever will. Distribute copies so parents can map their kids' routes to school and activities; mark the locations of their neighbors willing to help in an emergency.

• Organize a "buddy" network—again, teens can be really effective here—to call seniors, singles, and people with disabilities just to check in each day.

• Seniors and others who are at home most of the time can be "block watchers," watching for unusual activity on the street and looking out for children.

• Newspaper carriers, cab drivers, utility employees, and open-air merchants can be trained to be on the alert for any trouble in the neighborhood.

• Find out who has a talent for art (signs or posters announcing that yours is a neighborhood that won't tolerate crime), for gardening (convert that vacant lot), or for construction (repair and cleanup), and get these folks to give a little of their skill to the neighborhood. Think of everything and find a volunteer—we've all got special talents.

• Just getting out, working and playing outside, is a crime deterrent. Friendly neighbors and visible activity are crime's nemesis.

• Follow through with a full-fledged Neighborhood Watch group—your local police can help get you started, and so can the National Crime Prevention Council. See #4, Ask McGruff. For a neighborhood that says it cares, safety is a reachable goal.

STAND BY ME

Victim support goes a long way to fight crime

If it seems to you that fighting crime is something you can do only BEFORE it happens, think again. Criminals of all kinds walk free every day because a victim, already traumatized by the crime itself, can't find the strength to go through the additional stress of a court trial. Crime robs its victims of their sense of safety and control and can cause serious physical, financial, and

> CRIME VICTIMS ARE NOT SOMEONE
> ELSE. THEY ARE ALL OF US. VICTIM
> ASSISTANCE IS AN ESSENTIAL PART OF
> CRIME RESISTANCE.

psychological problems. Your support and concern is a POWERFUL act toward helping victims heal and stopping crime. Remember that victims are also witnesses, but more importantly they are our friends and neighbors.

If we expect to turn the tide and take control back from the creeps and hoodlums, we've got to take a stand at the side of the victims, understanding that what happens to another has EVERYTHING to do with you.

SIMPLE THINGS TO DO:

• Help victims with the immediate practical matters. Repair damage or take over child care. Offer to stay with a victim or to locate family or temporary shelter. Arrange for shopping, cooking, transportation, and other activities that are part of a victim's normal life. Help to reinforce both physical security in the victim's home and your neighborhood's concern and watchful protection.

• Most victims, male or female, will go through predictable stages of emotion—shock and denial, anger, powerlessness, guilt and depression—all normal and healthy. Listen without blame or questions. Understand that some victims need to talk about their experience over and over again, while others don't want to talk at all. Keep opinions or anger to yourself—this is not about you. Assure victims it is not their fault.

• Offer to accompany a victim to court, to the police, to the doctor, to essential services. Help victims get property returned, collect compensation, get access to counseling.

• Do not tolerate attitudes that blame victims for the crimes against them: "She asked for it" or "What did he expect, hanging around a place like that?" Speak out.

• Get information on victim services in your area. Ask police, the district attorney's office, and local mental health agencies how you can be a part of the local victim support network.

• Also contact the National Organization for Victim Assistance at 1-800-TRY-NOVA or the National Victim Center at 1-800-627-6872 or 1-703-276-2880 for information.

I WITNESS

Take the stand on the side of justice

Unreported and unprosecuted crime is a serious problem for many reasons. The criminal is not only allowed to get away with it but is almost certain to target someone else next. The victim remains a victim and misses an important step in regaining a sense of control. And we all lose because the police and courts can't do what we ask them to do.

We can help make our own lives safer by standing

AVOIDING CRIME IS WHAT WE ALL
WANT, BUT WHEN IT HAPPENS, MAKE A
DECISION TO TAKE A STAND
AGAINST IT.

firm—against the people who commit crime and beside the victims who suffer from it.

SIMPLE THINGS TO DO:

• If you observe a crime or if it happens to you, be alert to what you observe and make mental notes of what you see and hear—it will help you maintain your presence of mind as well as helping police later.

• Report a crime immediately—time is a key factor in apprehending a criminal, and even a few minutes' delay can mean his escape.

• While you're waiting for police to arrive, review what happened and make notes of every detail you can remember about the people—face, hair, clothing, marks, height, and weight, and about cars, weapons, etc., which may have been involved.

• Regardless of the nature of the crime and even if it does not involve personal contact—for example, a burglary when no one was around—the sense of being victimized can be overwhelming. If you are a victim, call someone to be with you. If you know a victim, make yourself available for support. See #48, Stand by Me.

• Understand that victims often feel the temptation to simply drop the matter, forget it, and move on. Consider that in the end it is worth it to prosecute.

• Be willing to testify and give your support to others who do. Many communities start a Court Watch group—people who accompany victims and witnesses to court and also are present regularly to remind the court that the community cares how it performs its job.

• We hear alarming stories of witnesses who refuse to testify because of fear of retaliation by criminals. Give your support and protection to innocent people who face this problem, and pressure government to provide better funding for witness protection.

• Teach children that it is up to each individual, not just "the system" and not just "others," to take positive action by reporting and testifying against crime.

◇ |50| ◇

PARTNER WITH POLICE

And other best friends

As a nation, we have been accused of refusing responsibility almost categorically, of expecting government to take care of us, and police to protect us. Whether or not this is true overall, we must realize that police can't be all places at once and that we share in the responsibility for our own well-being in every way.

Protecting yourselves and your property begins with simple things: reading this book and others, gathering family or neighbors together to solve common problems, devoting a Saturday to easy, inexpensive home improvements, writing local lawmakers to express your concerns, and changing our attitudes about government's role in crime prevention, about victims, about one another.

When we see the police and other services as our partners in fighting crime and work together with them to ensure the criminal justice system performs as it should, everybody wins.

WE ARE RESPONSIBLE FOR ENSURING
THAT OUR PERSONAL PROPERTY, OUR
HOMES AND BUSINESSES, AND OUR
FRIENDS AND FAMILIES ARE THE
SAFEST THEY CAN POSSIBLY BE. WE
CAN DO IT BEST BY WORKING WITH
NEIGHBORS, POLICE, AND COMMUNITY
AGENCIES AS PARTNERS AND FRIENDS.

SIMPLE THINGS TO DO:

• Most adults remember being told to look for a police officer if ever we found ourselves in trouble. It's still good advice today. The men and women who enter law enforcement are committed to the public good—to our safety and the prosecution of criminals. The most important thing we can do to assist them is to develop attitudes that support the work they do. Think and speak well of police in your home and teach children those attitudes. Be certain young children can identify police and fire vehicles and personnel, pointing out differences from other kinds of uniforms. NEVER use police as a threat with children: "If you don't behave they'll take you to jail." Teach partnership.

• All police, sheriff, and fire departments have a

public information officer or unit. Invite them to neighborhood meetings and youth activities to get solid, "from the source" information on fighting crime locally. Arrange for neighborhood groups to visit police, and encourage police to hold "open house" events for the community. Invite a police officer to kids' events or scout meetings—you will "wow" your attendees.

• Ask officials and residents to use every means possible to get criminals out of local neighborhoods. Find less obvious ways, like enforcing housing codes, fire or health codes, antinuisance and antinoise laws, drug-free clauses in leases, and so on.

• We can be better assured of finding a police officer when we need one if we push for more patrols, especially foot patrols, in our neighborhoods. Encourage lawmakers to support "community policing," which is working wonders across the country.

• Gather the facts about local crime (see #46, Know Your Neighbor), and get started with your Neighborhood Watch now. Start a Court Watch group, too, and get involved in services and support of victims and witnesses.

• Use the services law enforcement provides. See #5, Call Operation ID, and #3, Survey the Scene. Ask what help is available in other ways.

• Build community in every way you can. Volunteer at school, at senior centers, at the library, in victim advocacy, in adult literacy, food banks, soup kitchens, conservation groups, hospitals, nursing homes, service organizations. Organize, not just specific anticrime groups but recreational programs, classes, job services, community gardens, crime-prevention classes, community forums. Enlist the help of untapped resources in the community—seniors, teenagers, even young children can take responsibility for some aspect of a program. Focus on solving problems together, not just reacting to crises. Together we can make a real difference.

AFTERWORD

◆

... ...
... ... Public ...

Every single expert I talked to agrees on a few simple
"truths" about crime prevention. They're worth repeating here:

First, crime prevention begins with our attitudes. It's
not just what we do but what we think that counts, and
in talking about crime, it's impossible to ignore the de-
visiveness and chauvinism still rampant in a country so
advanced in other ways. Thinking that separates "us"
from "them," whether the "them" is Asians, women,
Catholics, pro-choicers, or Republicans, has contrib-
uted to countless criminal acts and will likely continue
until we take a firm stand against it. Hate and crime are
close companions. If we begin with the assumption that
any intelligent person can overcome any prejudice,
then changing attitudes is a choice we can make at any
time.

Second, our greatest safety lies in community.
Knowing one another inevitably makes us care about
one another, and where people care, crime goes down.

Always. Building community creates an invisible protective barrier against crime, and it's the easiest, most pleasant, most effective thing we can do to fight it.

Third, there is something powerful about DOING even just one thing. One thing, of course, usually leads to another, and that is how we will take our lives back from crime—one way at a time. Don't just read about it. DO IT.

Those of us putting the *50 Simple Ways* into action are bound to learn more. I'm interested in hearing what you learn and may assemble the best of your tips into a future collection of more tips on making life safer from crime. Please send your ideas to:

> Susan Hull
> c/o Pocket Books Publicity Dept.
> 1230 Avenue of the Americas
> New York, NY 10020

About the Author

Susan Hull has been a community activist, writer, and marketing consultant for many years. She is an active volunteer against domestic violence and crime in the community in Washington State in which she lives.

STRONG ON DEFENSE

SURVIVAL RULES TO PROTECT YOU AND YOUR FAMILY FROM CRIME

Sanford Strong, a retired San Diego Police Department trainer and supervisor, who has made numerous media appearances, including *Oprah* and *Today*, shows you how to make tough-minded survival decisions.

It's a book you can't afford to live without.

SANFORD STRONG